INTRODUCING THE DOTS

READING & WRITING MUSIC FOR ROCK MUSICIANS

To Judith, who's not interested in all this stuff.

INTRODUCING THE DOTS

READING & WRITING MUSIC FOR ROCK MUSICIANS

by

DAVE STEWART

BLANDFORD PRESS
Poole Dorset

First published in the U.K. 1982 by
Blandford Press, Link House, West Street,
Poole, Dorset, BH15 1LL

Distributed in the United States by
Sterling Publishing Co., Inc.,
2 Park Avenue, New York, N.Y. 10016.

British Library Cataloguing in Publication Data

Stewart, Dave
Introducing the dots.
1. Musical notation
I. Title
781'.24 ML431

ISBN 0 7137 1125 6

Phototypeset in 12/14pt 'Monophoto' Times
by Oliver Burridge & Co. Ltd

Printed in Great Britain by Butler & Tanner Ltd.
Frome, Somerset

Contents

Introduction

Many young band members, and most rock musicians as a whole, seem not only disinterested in being able to read and write music, but even a little scared of the idea. I can understand why really. After all, rock music is supposed to be fun and spontaneous and so on, and you can make a really exciting noise with your guitar without having to bother with all that

stuff. I mean, it's all down to *feel*, isn't it? All that reading music is what they used to try to get you to do in boring old school music lessons, anyway if you've got a really tight rhythm section and the band's really cooking, well, like, WHOOO! man, (etc, etc) twang blare . . . (fade).

Yes, yes, I know all about that and I agree with it to a certain extent. I think music should be fun, and what makes it that way is not so much the musicians' analytical knowledge of what they are playing, but more the instinctive feeling that goes into the music. But the ability to read and write can and should enhance this feeling, not detract from it. My theory is:

1 The best rock music is made by bands as opposed to solo musicians. The interplay that happens in really good groups is what makes them exciting to listen to.

2 Bands do need an internal system of communication to get ideas across to each other, so this interplay can begin to happen. If the guitarist writes a song, he has to be able to explain the chords and melody to the rest of the band.
Sorry if this seems painfully obvious so far, but the crux of it is:

3 The best system of internal communication for a group trying to play anything but the most basic ideas is the standard music notational system.

When you start playing in a band, it's usually E and A and D. You don't need to write that down. E for a bit, then up to A. Then kind of end on E again. But after a while you start getting your F minors and your B♭7s. That's when the trouble starts. Was it F6 for 7 bars, or E7 for 6 bars? At this point people usually jot down chord symbols on a piece of paper for reference, but this system doesn't work for writing down a melody. If you happen to know the notes in the tune, you can always write G A B D or whatever, but this tells you nothing about the rhythm of the melody or whether it starts very high or very low, etc.

There is an argument that says that after a few plays or listens you can remember songs and arrangements so you don't really need to write them down. Perhaps that is so, but it's surprising what you can forget in a week, let alone a year. Rather than spending all your money on a tape recorder to immortalise your band's latest compositions, why not buy a pencil and a few sheets of *manuscript* (= music writing) paper and learn to write them down? In this book I'm trying to explain how music notation works so that you will be able to read and write your melodies. I will deal with notes, rhythm and chords, and show how this applies to guitarists, bass guitarists, keyboard players and drummers as well as the general application to other instrumentalists, singers, and non-playing composers.

You may still think that all this is irrelevant to rock'n'roll—in which case I would add this—that being able to read and write music is no big deal. In fact, it's rather easy once you've learnt a few simple rules. If you can do it, it doesn't necessarily make you a better player than someone who can't, and I don't think there should be any status attached. It's just that if you are really interested in how and why music works, and want to be able to communicate quickly to other musicians, notation can only help you. It definitely won't make you any *worse* at what you do, it won't change your instinctive feel for your music (honest!), but it will enable you to understand better what you are trying to do. Once mastered, you'll find it a very useful asset . . .

. . . shall we proceed?

1 The Notes

This is a stave, on which we write the notes. The higher the pitch of the note, the higher its position on the stave. For example, [stave] is higher than [stave]

If the stave has this symbol 𝄞 at the beginning, it is used for the *treble* register, ie fairly high notes.

𝄞 is called the *treble clef*.

Here are the names of the notes on the treble stave:

on the lines, and:

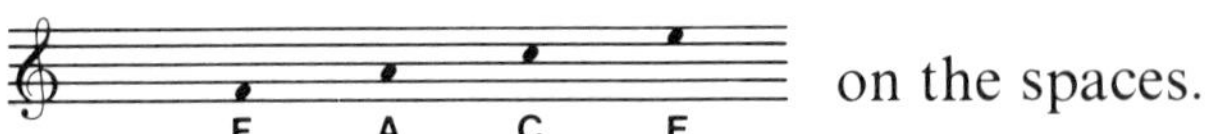

on the spaces.

when combined.

It is possible to go higher or lower, for example: F E D

and:

and if we want to write down further extremes, we use *leger* lines.

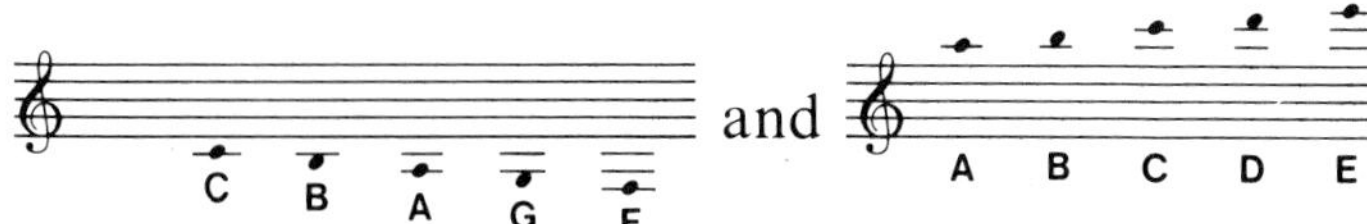

As depicted, leger lines are used to temporarily expand the range of the stave. Here is the complete range of the treble stave:

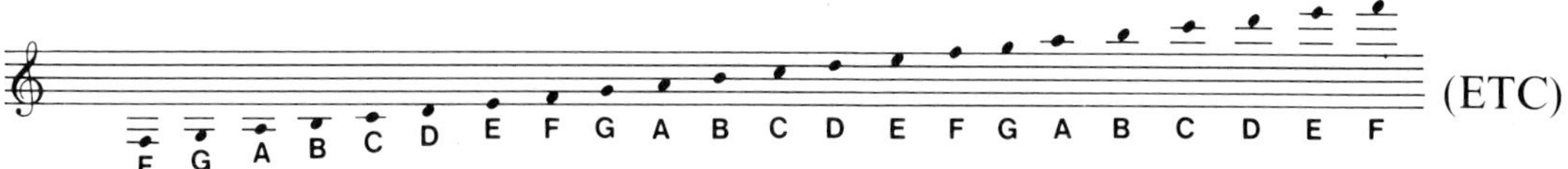

Notice that only the letters A, B, C, D, E, F, and G are used. (No Hs, please.)

The distance between the 1st and 2nd A is called an *octave*.

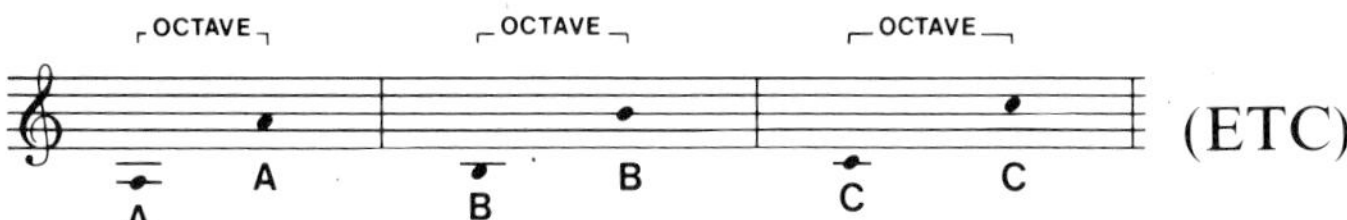

(ETC)

The range of notes available on the treble stave is sufficient to cover the range of guitars, flutes, voices, clarinets etc., but for lower instruments like the bass guitar we have to use the bass clef,

which looks like this: 𝄢

This is written at the beginning of the stave in the same way as the treble clef. Unfortunately the notes on it are all different.

on the lines, and:

on the spaces.

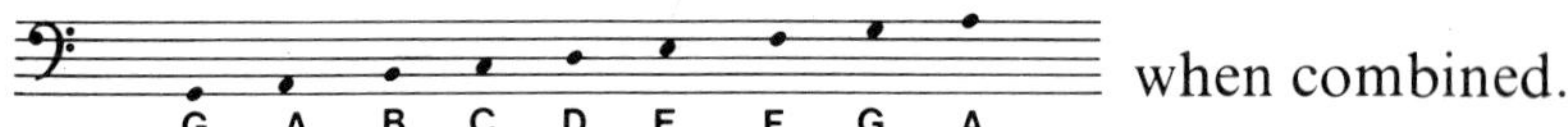

when combined.

The bass clef can have leger lines too:

F E D C B A

and:

When you get as high up as the C marked * on the bass stave, you overlap with the treble clef.

The note: can also be written:

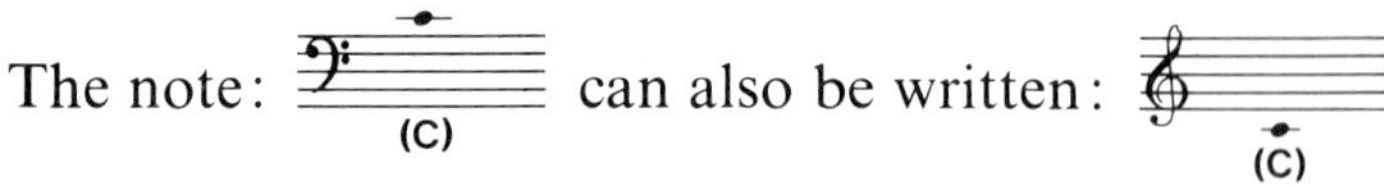

and is called *Middle C*. Middle C is a nice kind of medium note, neither too high nor too low. Numerologists and other students of the cosmic will be fascinated to learn that it vibrates at approximately 256 beats a second.

Combining the notes on both staves gives us the following diagram:

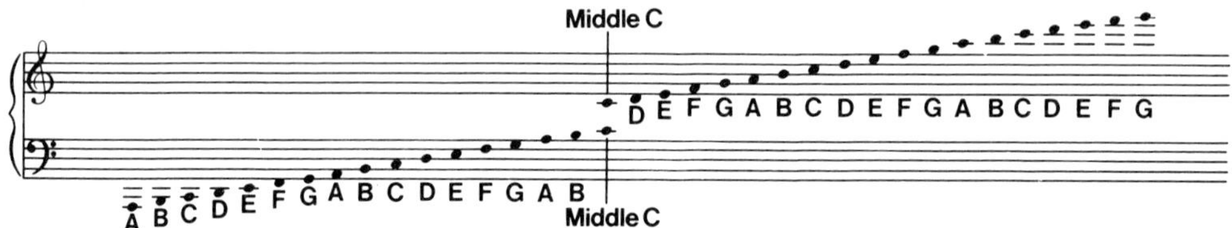

Please learn all these notes off by heart, as between this chapter and the next I shall personally visit all of your homes and set you a short but terrifying examination on note recognition. Having familiarised yourself with the written positions of the notes, you may well be wondering where to find them on your instruments, and, in the longer chapter that follows this is revealed. Turn to it with all possible haste.

2 Where to find the Notes

To begin to find the positions of notes on your instruments, let's start with the piano keyboard:

You see that the black notes are divided into alternate groups of two and

three. To find a note of C on the piano, pick one of the  type groups

and play the white note just to the left, ie: 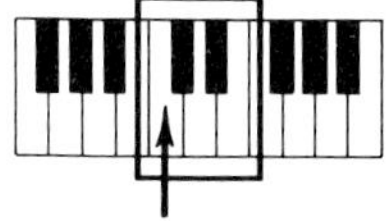

This is the note of C. It doesn't matter which end of the piano you play it, it's still a C! The note we call Middle C is usually found near the lock of the

piano lid, and as you recall, is written: 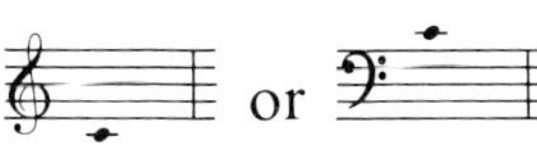

If we work upwards from C we arrive at D, E, F and G like this: 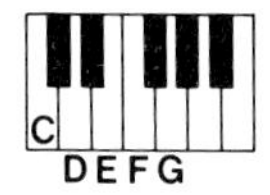

written:

C D E F G

The remaining two notes in the octave are A and B: 

written: A B

So on the piano (or any other keyboard instrument) the white notes are each represented by a letter.

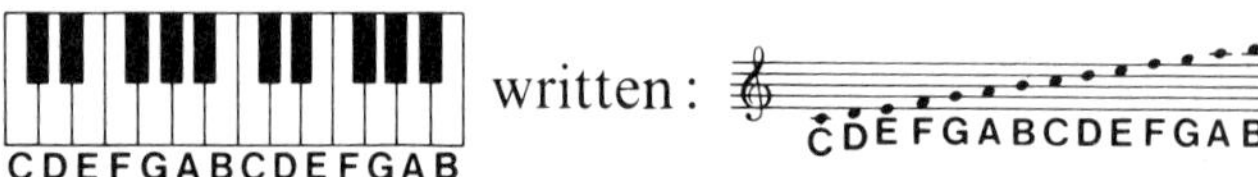

The black notes are the sharps and flats, which we'll come to in a minute, but first a brief explanation of note positions on the guitar.

The six strings of the guitar are tuned (from the bottom up) to the notes of E, A, D, G, B and E. If we represent these diagrammatically as

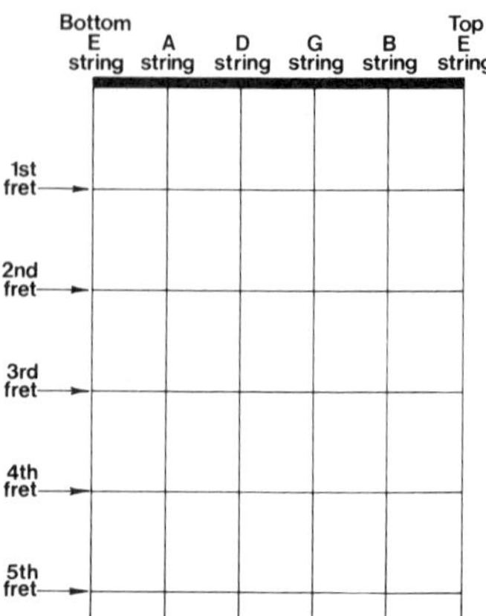

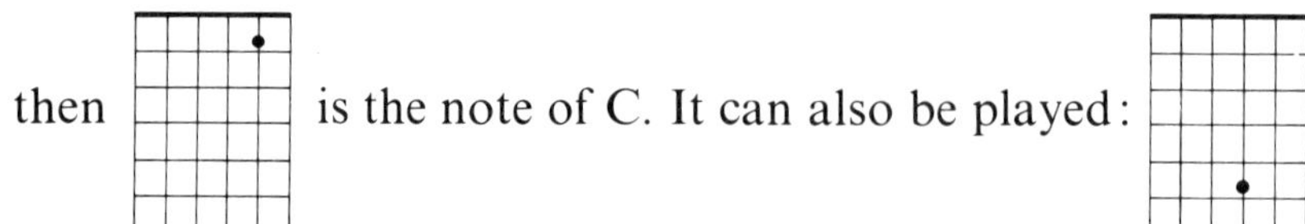

then is the note of C. It can also be played:

(and a couple of other ways too!) The other 'white' notes are:

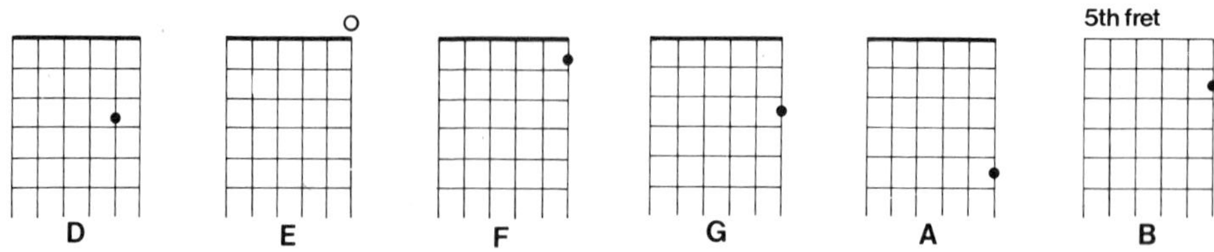

Of course there are other ways of playing these notes, ie:

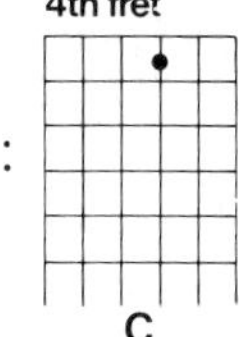

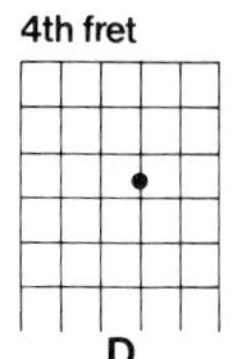

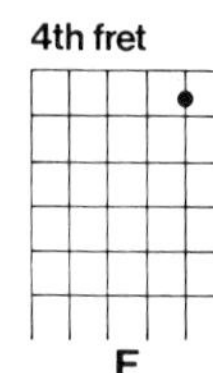

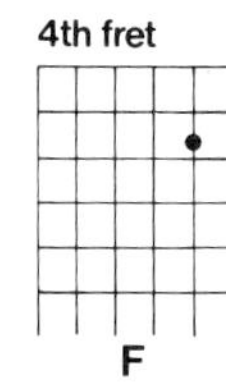

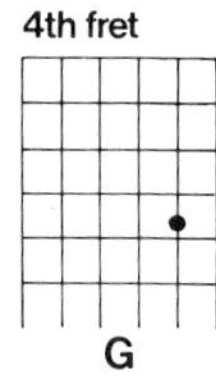

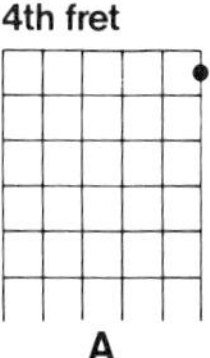

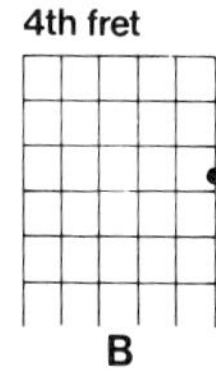

One slightly confusing thing about the guitar is that guitar music is written up one octave. This is to enable the whole range of the guitar to be written on the treble staff; so although the lowest note on the guitar (the bottom E string) sounds: when played,

in guitar music it will always be written:

which is one octave above its actual pitch. This places the guitar in the category of a *transposing* instrument (that is, an instrument whose played notes sound at a different pitch from those written) and saves the lucky guitarist from having to bother with the nasty bass clef. Not so the unfortunate bass guitarist, however, whose four strings are tuned (from the bottom up) E, A, D and G. These are written:

E A D G

but they actually sound like this:

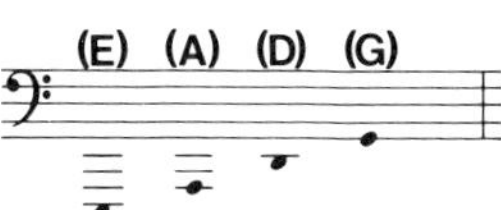

which means the bass guitar is also a transposing instrument, music for it being written one octave above its actual pitch. (This is to avoid the excessive use of leger lines, as notes like are a bit awkward to read.)

To find the seven principal notes on bass guitar it is necessary to follow these cunning diagrams:

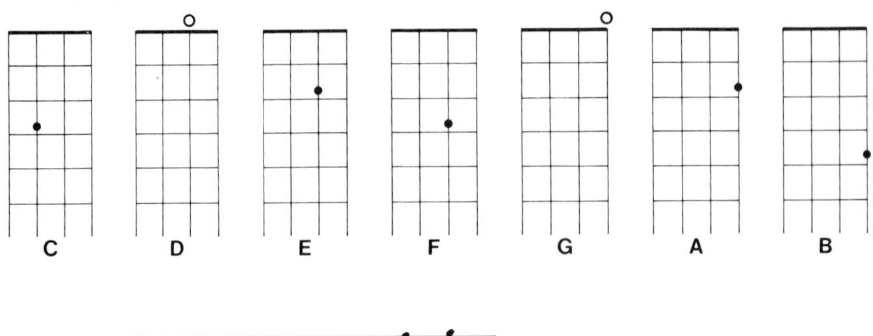

written: C D E F G A B

Now you know where A, B, C, D, E, F, and G are on your respective instruments. This really gives you all the notes you'll ever need except for the trifling matter of sharps and flats which we'll clear up in an instant. ♯ means sharp. ♭ means flat. *Sharp* means raised in pitch, higher. *Flat* means lowered in pitch. If a note is a flat, say for example a B flat, it means a B lowered in pitch by one semi-tone. (A *semi-tone* is the smallest interval you can use on a piano or a guitar. On the piano it is the distance between one key and its immediate neighbour(s) and on the guitar it is one fret's worth of distance.) So we arrive at B flat like this:

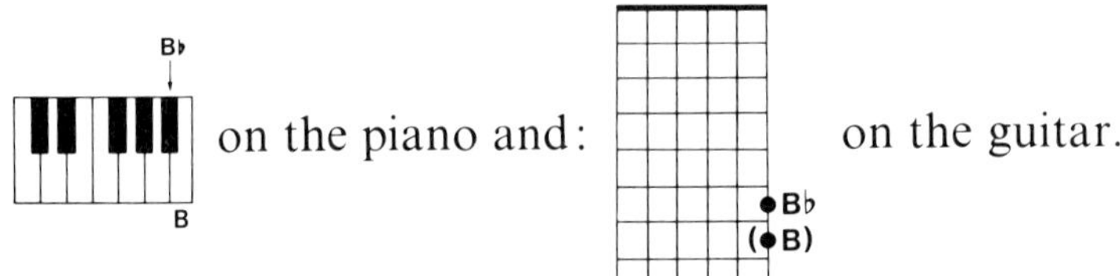

on the piano and: on the guitar.

Similarly A♭ is an A lowered in pitch by one semi-tone.

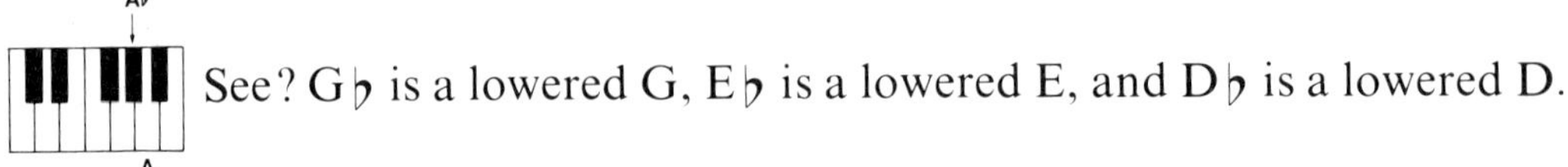

See? G♭ is a lowered G, E♭ is a lowered E, and D♭ is a lowered D.

Here are the flats: D♭E♭ G♭A♭B♭

Similarly a sharp raises the pitch of any note a semi-tone. C sharp is a raised C,

ie: 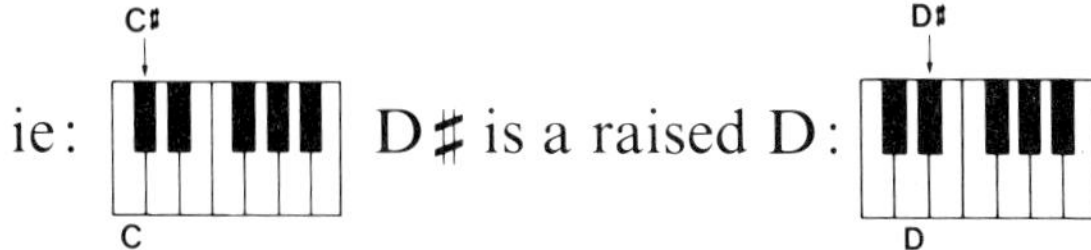

D♯ is a raised D:

Simple, innit? Stands to reason, dunnit? F♯ is a raised F, G♯ is a raised G

and A ♯ is a raised A. Voila les sharps: 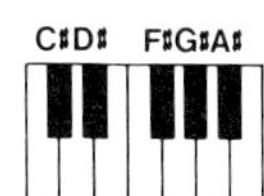

It may have occurred to some of you that F♯ and G♭ are the same note. You're right. There are times when one name is more apt than the other, but I'll save my explanation of this till chapter 5 by which time your musical IQ will be sufficiently raised for you to be able to grasp the concept with sneering ease. For now, suffice it to say that it is a matter of context . . . similarly you may have noticed that B♭ and A♯ are one and the same. It's true. Masters of disguise, these sharps and flats. It is also possible that you might come up against an F♭ one day. This is simply E by another name. And C♭ is plain old B. E♯ is F, and B♯ is C. Try not to let this confuse you! Even if you're not a keyboard player, it is worth having a look at the lay-out of the piano keyboard at this point, as it makes the flats and sharps picture fairly clear.

Here are the seven principal notes again: 

Here are the flats: 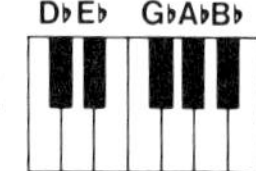

and here are the sharps: 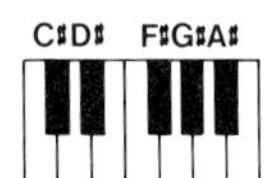

I'll end this chapter with some imposing looking diagrams to puzzle over. They show the names of the notes on each individual string of the guitar and bass guitar, and how to write these notes in notation form . . . also a summary of the positions of all the notes on the piano. Try to memorise as much of this as possible, as it's probably the key to the whole skill of reading and writing music.

Incidentally, notice that although we say F sharp and B flat (etc), in notation the accidental sign precedes the note name:

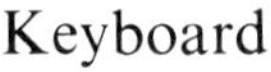

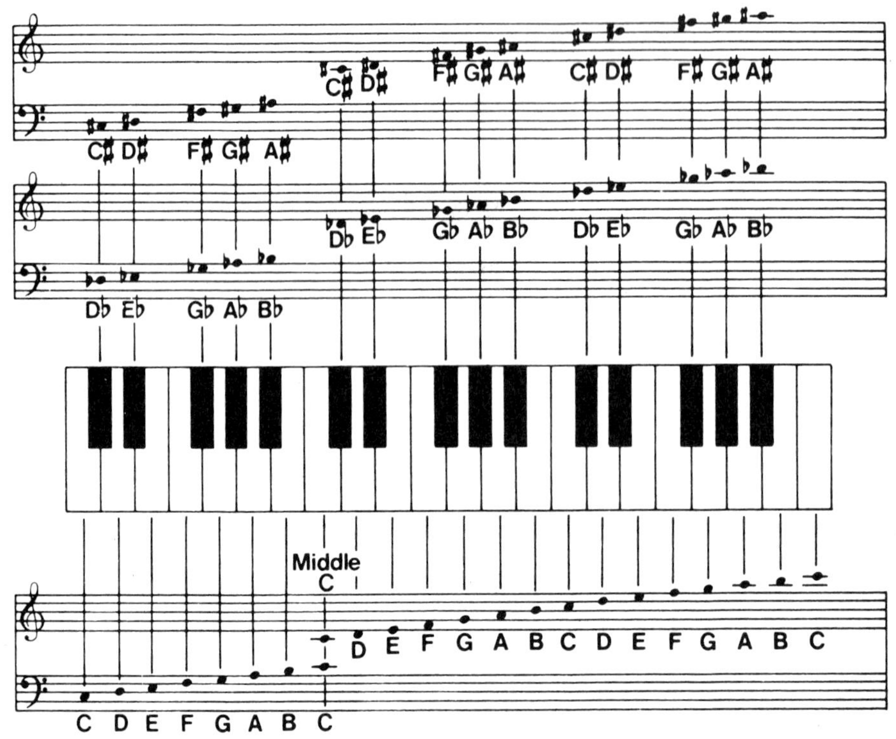

Next chapter: rhythm, the effect of bongos on white women, plus: irritatingly simple melodies and the beginnings of a more hopeful musical future.

---

6 string guitar

	E-string	A-string	D-string	G-string	B-string	E-string
Open string	E	A	D	G	B	E
1st fret	F	A♯ B♭	D♯ E♭	G♯ A♭	C	F
2nd fret	F♯ G♭	B	E	A	C♯ D♭	F♯ G♭
3rd fret	G	C	F	A♯ B♭	D	G
4th fret	G♯ A♭	C♯ D♭	F♯ G♭	B	D♯ E♭	G♯ A♭
5th fret	A	D	G	C	E	A
6th fret	A♯ B♭	D♯ E♭	G♯ A♭	C♯ D♭	F	A♯ B♭
7th fret	B	E	A	D	F♯ G♭	B
8th fret	C	F	A♯ B♭	D♯ E♭	G	C
9th fret	C♯ D♭	F♯ G♭	B	E	G♯ A♭	C♯ D♭
10th fret	D	G	C	F	A	D
11th fret	D♯ E♭	G♯ A♭	C♯ D♭	F♯ G♭	A♯ B♭	D♯ E♭
12th fret (octave)	E	A	D	G	B	E
13th fret	F	A♯ B♭	D♯ E♭	G♯ A♭	C	F
14th fret	F♯ G♭	B	E	A	C♯ D♭	F♯ G♭

Bass guitar

	E-string	A-string	D-string	G-string
Open string	E	A	D	G
1st fret	F	A♯ B♭	D♯ E♭	G♯ A♭
2nd fret	F♯ G♭	B	E	A
3rd fret	G	C	F	A♯ B♭
4th fret	G♯ A♭	C♯ D♭	F♯ G♭	B
5th fret	A	D	G	C
6th fret	A♯ B♭	D♯ E♭	G♯ A♭	C♯ D♭
7th fret	B	E	A	D
8th fret	C	F	A♯ B♭	D♯ E♭
9th fret	C♯ D♭	F♯ G♭	B	E
10th fret	D	G	C	F
11th fret	D♯ E♭	G♯ A♭	C♯ D♭	F♯ G♭
12th fret (octave)	E	A	D	G
13th fret	F	A♯ B♭	D♯ E♭	G♯ A♭
14th fret	F♯ G♭	B	E	A

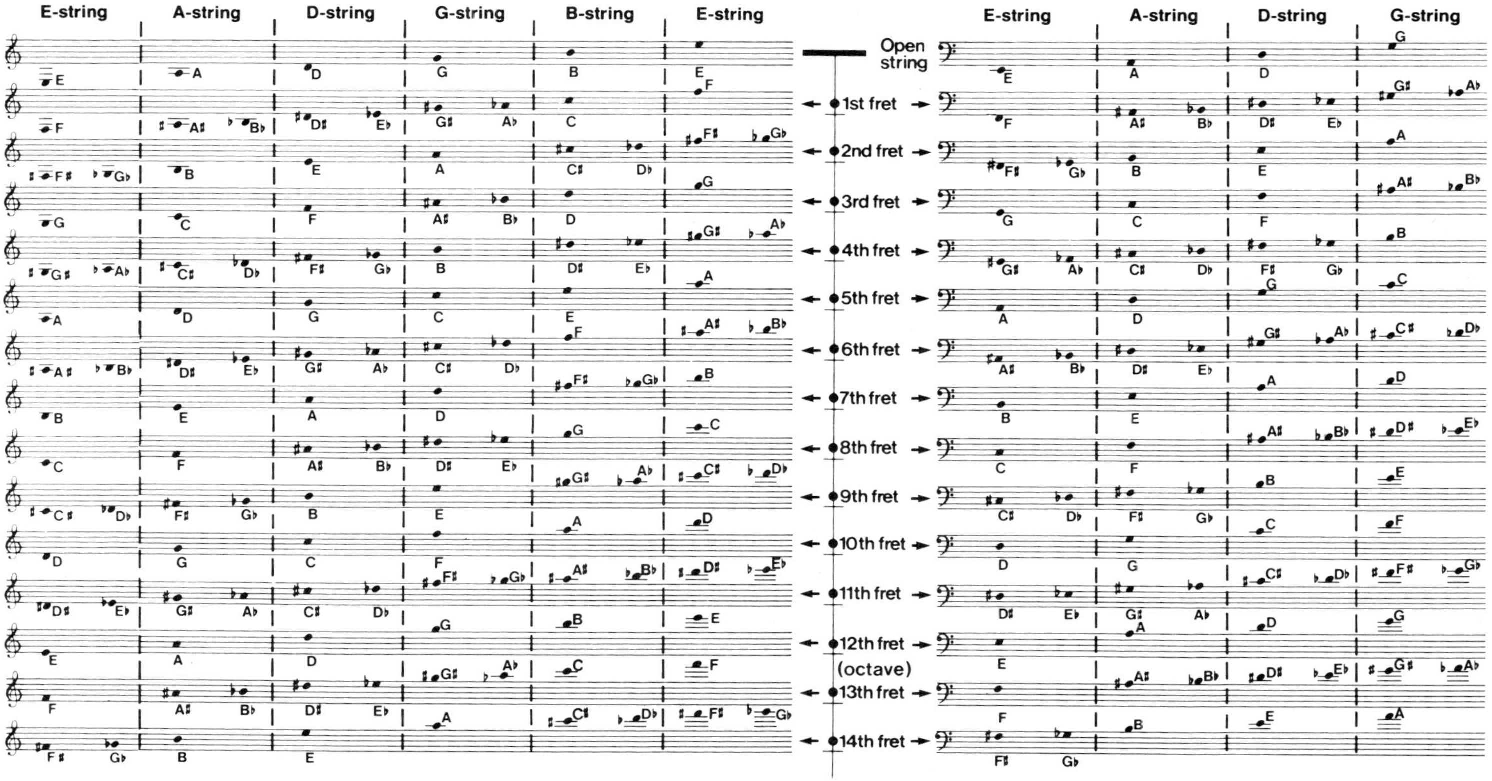

3 Rhythm I

A music writer called Phil Sutcliffe once wrote a review of a National Health gig in which he mentioned some of the funny time-signatures the band used, eg $\frac{33}{37}$. Now, Phil's a good writer and a nice guy, but what he wasn't to know is that (thankfully!) there is no such thing as $\frac{33}{37}$ time. Even if there was, I doubt that anyone would be able to play it. I hope Phil's reading this as I intend in the next two chapters to throw the whole immensely complex and baffling matter of rhythm into crystal clarity with a few pompous strokes of my pen.

Different length notes are written in different ways, and each has its own (often hilarious) name. For example, this type of note 𝅗𝅥 is a minim. This ♩ is a crotchet, and this ♪ is a quaver. Of the three, the minim (𝅗𝅥) is the longest. In each minim there are two crotchets 𝅗𝅥 → ♩ ♩

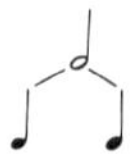

and in each crotchet, two quavers: ♩ → ♪ ♪

This gives us: 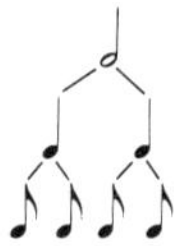 𝅗𝅥 → ♩ ♩ → ♪ ♪ ♪ ♪, a neat little hierarchy.

Given that, it follows that a minim is twice the length of a crotchet, and that a crotchet is twice the length of a quaver. It also follows that a minim is four times the length of a quaver.

Now this doesn't tell you anything about the speed or tempo of the notes, only their relative lengths. The tempo of a piece will usually be indicated by ♩ = 108 or ♪ = 100 or something like that. This simply means that in the first example there will be 108 crotchets per minute, and in the second 100 quavers per minute. Obviously if there are 108 crotchets a minute, there will be 54 minims, or 216 quavers. If the tempo were ♩ = 120, there'd be two crotchets every second.

For longer notes, we have 𝅝 , which is twice the length of a minim. 𝅝 is called a semibreve. Twice the length of a semibreve is a breve, written 𝅜 , though this is fairly rare.

For the shorter notes, we take the quaver (♪) and sub-divide it by adding 'tails': 𝅘𝅥𝅯 is a semiquaver (two in every quaver),

𝅘𝅥𝅰 is a demisemiquaver (two in every semiquaver)

and 𝅘𝅥𝅱 is a . . . wait for it . . .

hemidemisemiquaver.

That (thank heavens) is as far as it needs to go, because even at the slow tempo of ♩ = 60 a hemidemisemiquaver would be incredibly fast, 16 of them per second. No-one can actually play that fast accurately, so it is a bit irrelevant; but by all means amuse yourselves with thoughts of millimicroquavers and nanoquavers.

All this adds up to the pyramidal diagram below:

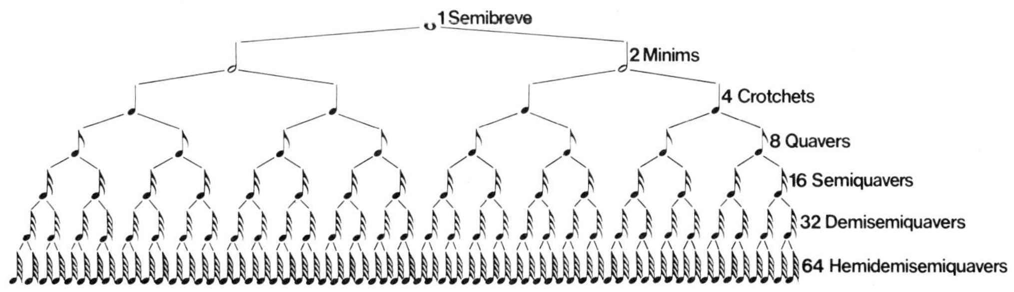

Consecutive quavers are often written with their 'tails' joined for visual neatness (eg ♫ instead of ♪♪ and ♬♬ instead of ♪♪♪♪).

This applies to semiquavers, demisemiquavers and hemidemisemiquavers as well:

American musicians don't like all this crotchet and quaver lark. To them ♩ is a quarter note, ♪ is an eighth note, etc. 𝅝 (a semibreve) is their whole note. In a way I suppose that's easier, but I rather like the names myself!

Going back to what I said earlier about $^{33}_{37}$ time; when you read or write a piece of music, there should always be a *time signature* indicated at the beginning. This takes the shape of two figures, one above the other (rather like a mathematical fraction but without the intervening line), which tells you how many beats there are in a bar and what type of beats they are (crotchets, quavers or minims etc). A bar is a rhythmic sub-division, marked out with bar lines:

The most common time signature is $^{4}_{4}$ (sometimes called *common time*), which consists of four crotchets per bar:

All time signature symbols are written in a sort of code; the bottom number tells you the *type* of beat, the code for crotchet being 4. The top number tells you *how many* of these beats there are in a bar. Therefore $^{4}_{4}$ means:

4 - Amount per bar
4 - Code for CROTCHET } 4 Crotchets per bar =

$\frac{3}{4}$ would mean three crotchets per bar:

and $\frac{5}{4}$ is five crotchets per bar:

Now the code for a quaver is 8, so a time signature of which the lower number is 8 tells you that there are so many quavers in a bar. $\frac{6}{8}$ means:

6-Amount per bar 8-Code for QUAVER } 6 Quavers per bar =

Similarly the code for a semiquaver is 16, and that of a demisemiquaver is 32. If you look back to the pyramidal diagram, it becomes clear that the code for minim has to be 2. So if you see a time signature like $\frac{3}{2}$, it means

three minims in every bar:

You don't have to be much of a mathematician to work out why $\frac{33}{37}$ time is an impossibility!

When looking at the bottom figure of a time signature, just remember this table:

2 = MINIM
4 = CROTCHET
8 = QUAVER
16 = SEMIQUAVER
32 = DEMISEMIQUAVER
64 = HEMIDEMISEMIQUAVER

If you bear in mind the 'code' explanation, it makes rhythms like $\frac{13}{8}$ seem a little little less intimidating. $\frac{13}{8}$ is simply 13 quavers per bar, which, while it might be a little hard to play at first, is certainly not difficult to understand.

One more thing about time signatures; in a lot of music (say, for example, *Three Blind Mice*, a wonderful historic tune which we all know and love) the time signature will remain the same throughout the piece. In the case of *Three Blind Mice* the time signature is $\frac{4}{4}$, and this will be written once, at the beginning of the piece, immediately after the clef and the key signature. All the bars thereafter will be $\frac{4}{4}$ bars; that is, adding up to four crotchets. In other types of music, though, the time signature may change during the piece, and may even differ from bar to bar. For example:

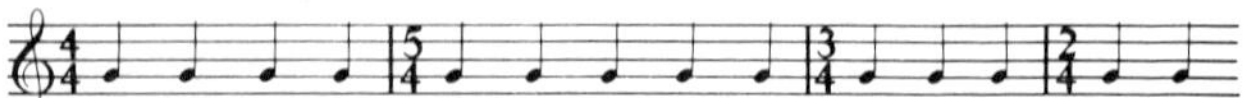

Each time the time signature changes it has to be indicated at the beginning of the bar. With consecutive bars of the same length, the time signature can be omitted:

So the time signature always applies to all ensuing bars unless contra-indicated.

Finally, don't be confused by what I have said about the 'code' system. A $\frac{4}{4}$ bar is basically a bar with four crotchets; however, that is not to say that it could not have eight quavers, or two minims. Or even six quavers and four semiquavers. As long as the total adds up to the *equivalent* of four crotchets, it will be a $\frac{4}{4}$ bar!

4 Rhythm II

Right, that's put Phil Sutcliffe straight. Now to continue with rhythm . . . there are two ways of increasing the rhythmic value of notes. The first is by *tying*. Let us say we wanted to have a note which lasted for five quavers. A semibreve (= eight quavers) is obviously too long to be helpful, but we can take a minim (= four quavers) and add the fifth quaver by tying it on.

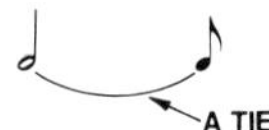

Or, if a note which lasted three quavers was needed, we could tie a crotchet (= two quavers) to another quaver.

Ties are very useful in that they can span bar lines:

and:

and by using them to tie together various types of notes, composite notes of any rhythmic value can be indicated.

The other way of increasing note-length is to use a dot. If you add a dot to a note (♩.) its value is increased by 50%.

The whole 'table' of dotted notes looks like this:

𝅝. = 𝅝 + 𝅗𝅥
𝅗𝅥. = 𝅗𝅥 + ♩
♩. = ♩ + ♪
♪. = ♪ + 𝅘𝅥𝅯
𝅘𝅥𝅯. = 𝅘𝅥𝅯 + 𝅘𝅥𝅰
𝅘𝅥𝅰. = 𝅘𝅥𝅰 + 𝅘𝅥𝅱

These are especially useful in 3-type time signatures like $\frac{3}{4}$, $\frac{6}{8}$, $\frac{12}{8}$ and $\frac{9}{8}$.

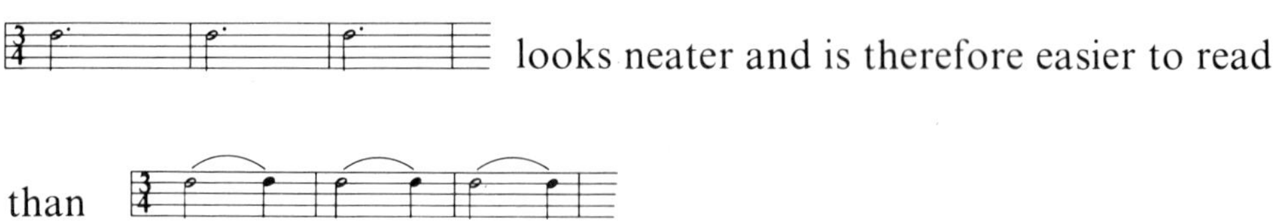

looks neater and is therefore easier to read than

Dots can be used in conjunction with ties as well:

Unfortunately dots cannot bridge bar lines in the same way as a tie:

is a mathematical impossibility (I hope you can see why!).

Really, rhythm is just a question of maths in many respects. Given a bar of fairly complex rhythmic structure, the best approach is to analyse it mathematically using your knowledge of note-lengths.

|$\frac{4}{4}$ 𝅗𝅥 ♩ ♩ | is a pretty simple grouping; one long note followed by two shorter ones. Most people can tap out four beats with their foot, and slap their thighs on beats 1, 3 and 4.

|$\frac{9}{8}$ ♩. ♩ ♪♩. | looks more intimidating, but can be worked out just as surely.

The foot taps out nine quaver beats (not necessarily very fast) and the thigh is slapped on beats 1, 4, 6 and 7. (Remember that the time signature doesn't indicate the *tempo*, only the type of bar.) Similarly, if you can hear a rhythm in your mind (or play a rhythm that you like) and want to write it down, try to reduce it to a mathematical formula. *Every* rhythm has some sort of beat running through it.

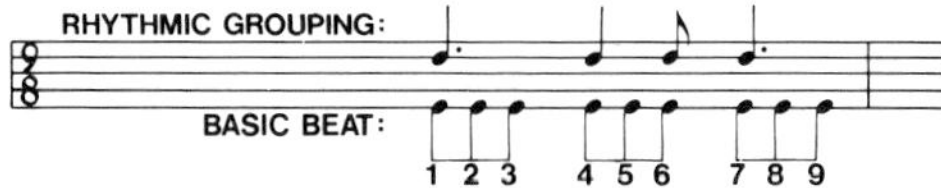

Try to play or tap out a series of equal beats and work out on which ones your particular rhythm falls. The foot-and-thigh method is particularly recommended by the author, and any number of medical preparations will bring fast, soothing relief to thighs badly chapped by a hard day's slapping out $\frac{63}{64}$ time.

Having glibly dismissed the entire question of musical rhythm as mere mathematics, and thus something which can be perfectly adequately worked out with pocket calculators, I would like to draw your flagging attention to *rests*. Rests are instructions not to play. Musicians working in West End theatres and night-spots are particularly fond of them, especially the ones that look like this: 112

Each note has its equivalent rest. A crotchet rest looks like this: 𝄽 .

When reading a bar like 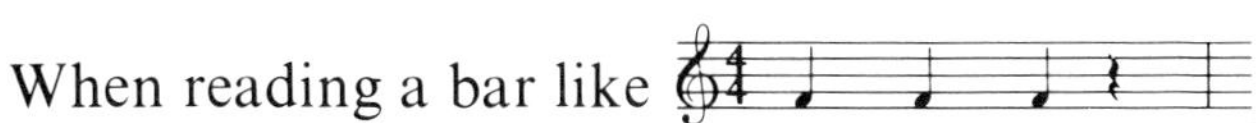

the first, second and third beats are played, and the fourth is silent. A quaver rest is 𝄾 , a semiquaver rest is 𝄿 .
Here are the rests written alongside their equivalent note:

𝅝	SEMIBREVE	𝄻
𝅗𝅥	MINIM	𝄼
𝅘𝅥	CROTCHET	𝄽
𝅘𝅥𝅮	QUAVER	𝄾
𝅘𝅥𝅯	SEMIQUAVER	𝄿
𝅘𝅥𝅰	DEMISEMIQUAVER	𝅀
𝅘𝅥𝅱	HEMIDEMISEMIQUAVER	𝅁

Rests can be dotted in the same way as notes, and again the dot adds 50% to the value.

So in a bar of $^{12}_{8}$, we might see:

or:  or even:

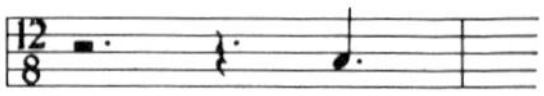

The semibreve rest ( ) doubles as an all-purpose whole bar's rest, ie

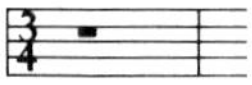

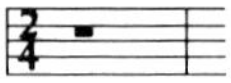

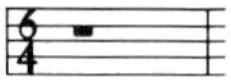

In a piece where the time signature varies a lot, this is convenient, as:

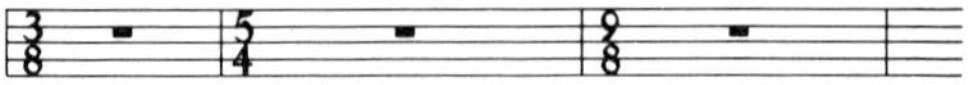

looks much neater than:

and is much less likely to confuse someone reading a part. For long rests, say 32 bars silence, 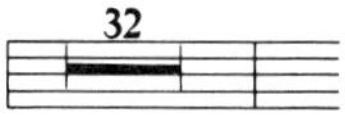 32 to save space. The expression *tacet* (Latin for 'shut up') is also used to indicate silence, as in 'tacet for 32 bars'.

As I've mentioned, when writing groups of notes like quavers or semiquavers, the 'tails' are often joined:  rather than:

In a rhythm involving the use of crotchets, the smaller notes will often be joined in *crotchet groups*, ie

This can get more complex: ♬♪ is an abbreviation for ♬♪ and ♪♬ is an abbreviation for ♪♬

♬♪ can be written ♬♪

Sometimes rests are included, as in ♬ (=♬)

Dots can occur, ♪. ♬ (=♪. ♬) and ♬ ♪. (=♬ ♪.)

Joining the tails in this way means that the notes can be seen as a block, and as these blocks correspond to the beat of the bar, it makes reading a little easier.

is a lot more manageable than:

Finally, triplets. These are written ♫ or ♩♩♩ (etc), and signify three notes to be played in the space of two.

♩♩♩ are three equal notes played in the space of ♩ ♩, called a 'crotchet triplet'. A 'minim triplet' is written 𝅗𝅥𝅗𝅥𝅗𝅥 and signifies three equal notes played in the space of two minims . . . and so on.

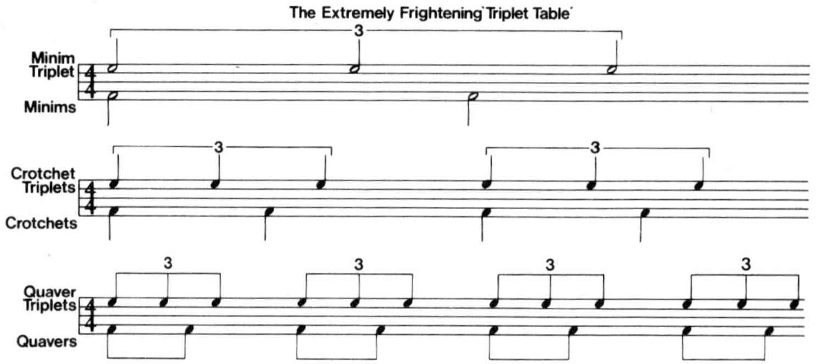

Occasionally triplets will occur inside a 'crotchet group',

eg 

Actually these quicker triplets, although they look a bit menacing, are far easier to play than the slow ones.

Far harder is to play a slow triplet like [4/4 minim triplet, 3] accurately.

(Try it and see!)

5 Key Signatures

You are, I take it, by now thoroughly versed in the principles of rhythm—which have been explained to you in the last two chapters with laborious exactitude. In addition, I trust you have earnestly continued to swot over chapter 2, which explained with dogged patience the names of the notes and their secret hiding-places on your instruments. By keeping a clear head, it should be possible for you to combine these two elements which I have generously taken the time and trouble to outline, and produce TUNES and MELODIES from your wretched banjos and accordions. I don't have to do this, you know. I could have been a nuclear physicist . . .

When you see a melody written down, the first symbol given is the clef.

𝄞 is the treble clef, 𝄢 the bass clef.

The next indication is the *key signature* (if any). This tells you what sharps or flats are going to occur throughout the piece, which in turn tells you what key the piece is in. For example:

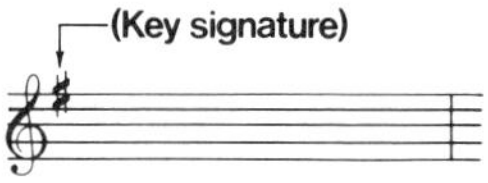

(Key signature)

This example, a sharp sign on the F line, means that all Fs in the piece will be sharp unless contra-indicated by a *natural* sign.

A natural sign (♮) written in front of a note in the same way as a sharp or flat sign:

cancels any previous instructions and makes the note its 'natural' self.

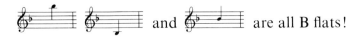

Another common key signature is meaning that all Bs will be flat throughout the piece. Incidentally, the *accidental* sign (ie sharp or flat) used in a key signature applies to the named note in *any* position on the stave—so

and are all B flats!

The reason for using a key signature is that it saves having to write in the accidental each time it occurs. The only problem for the reader is then to *remember* that all Fs are sharp, all Bs and Es are flat, or whatever. However, this soon becomes second nature when the accidentals of each key are learnt.

signifies the key of G major. This has only one accidental, the F♯. Try playing the eight notes of the G major scale on your Sootyphone, banjo, or Oberheim 8-voice polyphonic synthesiser:

Got it? These two accidentals: signify the key of D major,

the scale of which is:

A piece with no key signature indicated means one of two things; either it is in the key of C major, with no accidentals whatsoever:

or else it is the sort of piece where there is no fixed key, and the writer prefers to write in the accidentals as they occur. Here is a table of most of the major keys and the scales thereof:

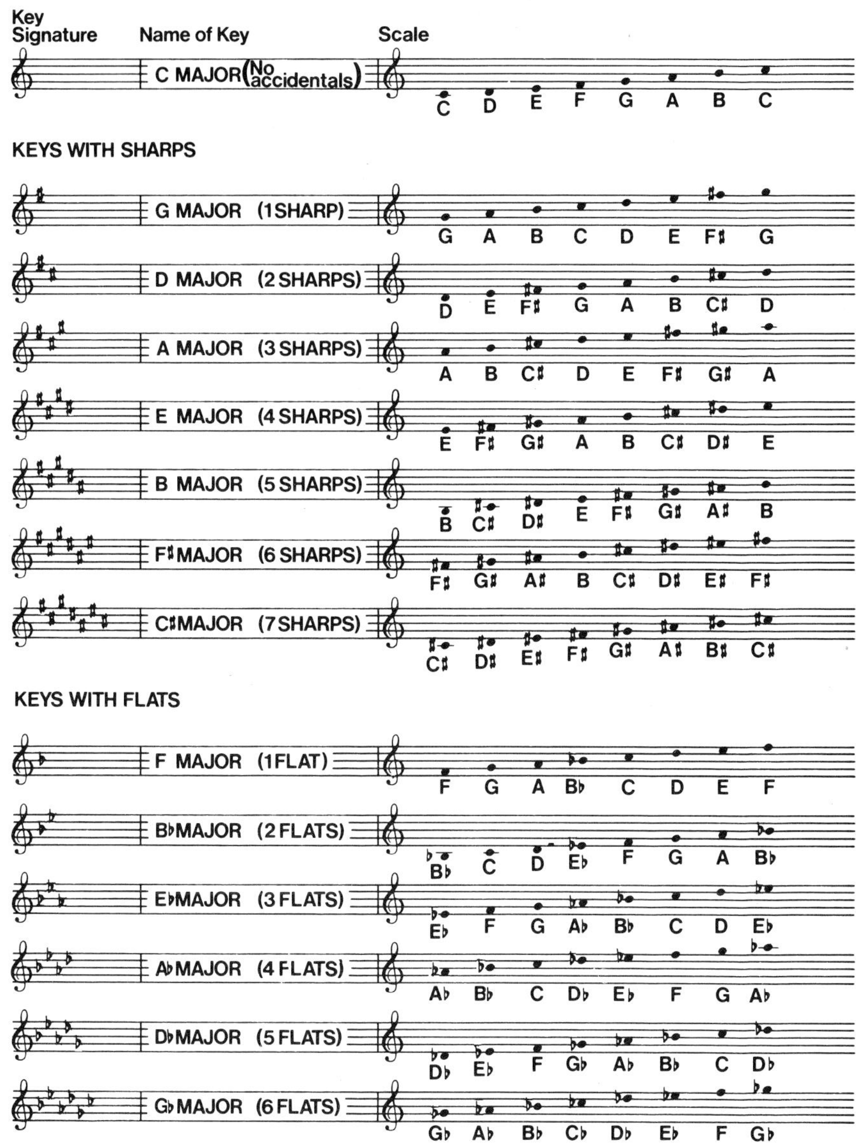

Notice that in the keys of F♯, C♯ and G♭ major some esoteric notes like E♯, B♯ and C♭ occur. Remember that E♯ = F, B♯ = C, and C♭ = B! The reason for adopting what might seem a rather unnecessary accidental is to preserve the *visual shape* of the written scale.

is a far less satisfactory way of writing the scale of

F♯ major than

because the 'shape' of the former is wrong. In order to satisfy the eye, a major scale when written should look like

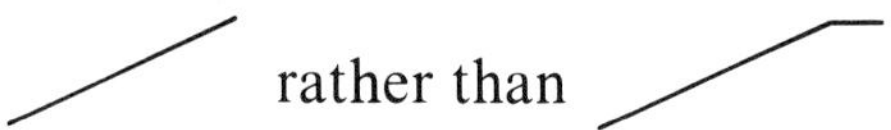

To achieve this smooth ascent, the note name has to change at each of the seven steps of the scale. Two Fs (one an F♮, the other an F♯) at the end of the first example of the F♯ major scale give a false sense of 'sameness' to the two notes and spoil the shape of the rising scale: E♯ and F♯ (although of course sounding exactly the same as F♮ and F♯) are more obviously different notes . . . Think about it!

You may have noticed that there are some possible major scales, for example G♯ major and D♯ major, which are omitted from your table. The reason for this is a new terror which, so far, I have been reluctant to reveal to you, but now I fear there is no alternative. In order to preserve the correct shape of some major scales (and adhere to the principle of the note name having to change at each step of the scale) it is sometimes necessary to use *double flats* and *double sharps*. A double flat (written ♭♭) lowers the pitch of a note by a *whole tone* (groan). In other words, A♭♭ = G (shriek).

A double sharp (written 𝄪) raises the pitch of a note by a whole tone (howl). G𝄪 = A (sob).

I'm really sorry about this. Many of you may by now have decided that music is an unsuitable career after all, or have thrown the book into a far corner of the room in a vain attempt to banish from your minds this new piece of insufferable academicism. However, it does make sense. If you try to write the scale of D♯ major without using double sharps, the result is:

With double sharps, it looks like this:

Shape:

(Fab)

—notice how the note name changes at each step of the scale in the latter instance.

There are also examples where double flats can be similarly usefully employed, but let us leave that for now. They are not common enough to warrant too much anxiety at this stage.

Some Notes on Key Signatures:

1 Where a natural sign is used to cancel an accidental indicated by a key signature (for example), the natural sign is only effective for the duration of the bar in which it occurs. After this bar, the key signature accidentals come into force again. If (in the previous example) an F♮ were needed in the second bar as well as the first, it would have to be written in again.

This also applies to additional accidentals. If the key signature were

(ie key of D major) and a G♯ was needed in one bar—

the sharp sign would only affect Gs in *that bar*. The same is true of flats, double flats and double sharps.

2 A whole key signature can be *cancelled* by utilising the appropriate natural signs.

and:

Note how, in the last example, the F♯ is cancelled, then re-introduced as an accidental in the new key.

3 In a key signature, sharps and flats are never intermingled, but kept apart in a sort of enharmonic apartheid. If you wanted to write a melody out in the key of D major, it would be wrong (or at least, misleading) to

write (G♭, C♯) as an indication of the key signature;

(F♯, C♯) is the accepted way.

Configurations like or do not occur, as they do not represent a major scale of any key.

6 Intervals/Chords I

The distance between any two notes is described in musical terms as an *interval*. These intervals describe exactly the difference in pitch between two notes; for example, the interval of middle C and the G above it is known as a *Perfect 5th*. Taking the scale of C major as a simple example, here are the names of the intervals:

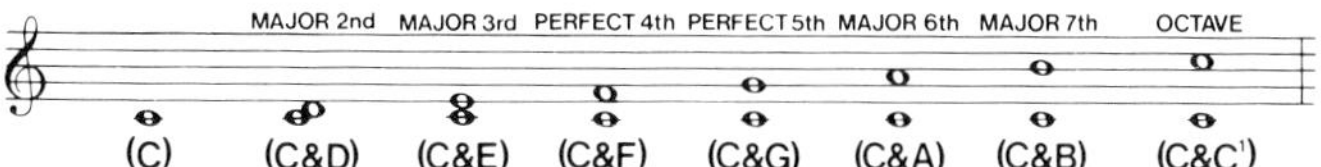

After the octave, we can continue:

MAJOR 9th (C&D') MAJOR 10th (C&E') PERFECT 11th (C&F') PERFECT 12th (C&G') MAJOR 13th (C&A')

After that it is simpler to say 'an octave plus a major 7th' etc. We could in fact describe a major 9th as an octave plus a major 2nd, a major 10th as an octave plus a major 3rd, etc. The choice is really a matter of personal preference.

It helps to have a good understanding of these intervals, as they form the basis of chords. I think it is virtually impossible to have a good chord sense and be able to find interesting voicings from chords unless you can recognise and appreciate the intervals working within the chord—but more of this later.

There are, of course, other intervals hiding in between the ones I've already shown you. So much to learn, so little time . . .

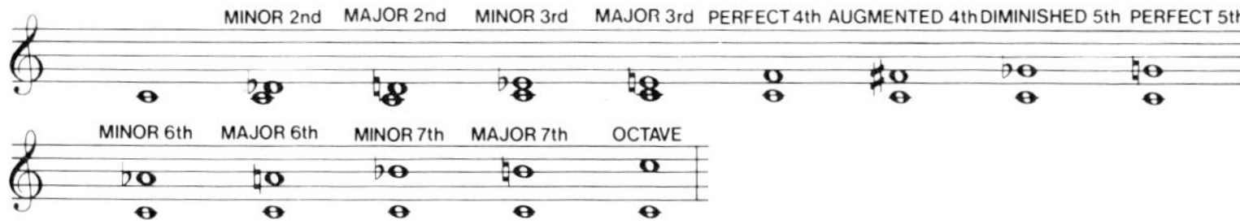

We have used our old friend 'C' again here as the reference point, but these interval names apply whatever the starting note. Another example:

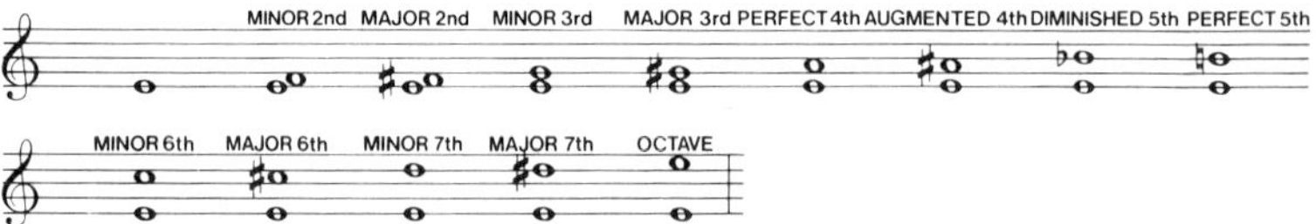

Get it? Guitarists may find this sort of thing a little easier than pianists, as they can calculate each interval in terms of numbers of frets.

Minor 2nd	1 fret
Major 2nd	2 frets
Minor 3rd	3 frets
Major 3rd	4 frets
Perfect 4th	5 frets
Augmented 4th Diminished 5th }	6 frets
Perfect 5th	7 frets
Minor 6th	8 frets
Major 6th	9 frets
Minor 7th	10 frets
Major 7th	11 frets
Octave	12 frets
(etc)	

Pianists may initially have a harder time memorising intervals on their instruments, as the layout of the keyboard gives rise to visual discrepancies. For example, a perfect fifth can be two white notes (C & G), two black notes (E♭ & B♭), or a combination (B♭ & F). Of course they all sound like fifths, but the difference in the visual patterning often serves to confuse the young nervous player groping desperately at the keys. Don't let me put you off, though.

I think it's about time we had a quick quiz to liven up this book. See if you can work out the names of these intervals:

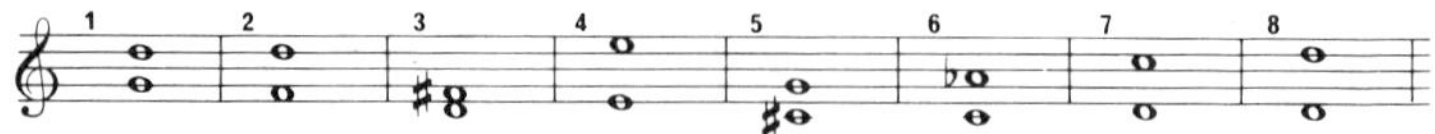

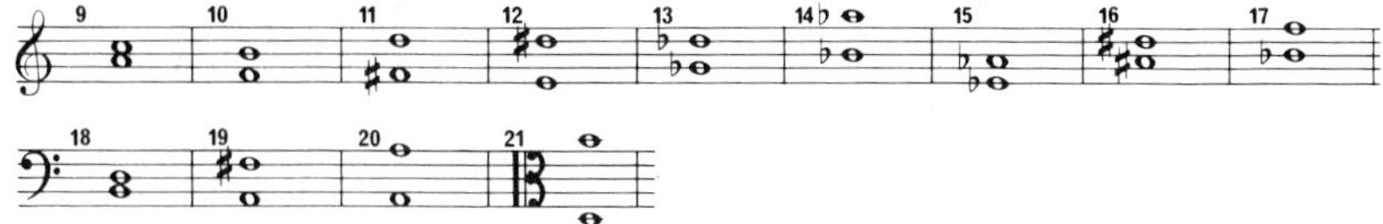

(Answers on p. 41.)

Unfortunately the budget for this book does not stretch to offering pink Cadillacs, recording contracts or weekends with the star of your choice (either sex) as incentive prizes for the lucky interval-guesser, but curb your disappointment and let your consolation be that you are adding bit by bit to your paltry musical knowledge. Anyone getting no. 21 has cheated and read the last chapter first, shame on you!

And now, the part you've all been waiting for. You loved the sharps and flats; you roared at the time signatures; you wept unashamedly at the antics of the little semiquavers, howled in terror at the awful double flats and micturated with mirth over the $\frac{33}{37}$ syncopations. Now, from the same team that brought you all this, comes—

Chords—Major and Minor

Any three notes played simultaneously constitute a chord. The major chord

is the simplest:

The name of a chord is determined by its ingredients, the three (or more) notes within it. The exact position of these three notes is not important as regards establishing the name of the chord. C, E and G make up a chord of 'C major', and can be played:

or: or: or: or even

As long as these three notes are represented somehow within the chord, it will be called C major. The three most common positions of this chord (on piano) are:

and ,

all of which can be played comfortably with one hand. These 3-note chords are often referred to as *triads*, meaning a set of 3 notes which make up a major or minor chord.

Looking back to the intervals explained earlier, you will note that the three ingredients are: **1** Key note or *root*, **2** Major 3rd, **3** Perfect 5th. This is true of all major chords:

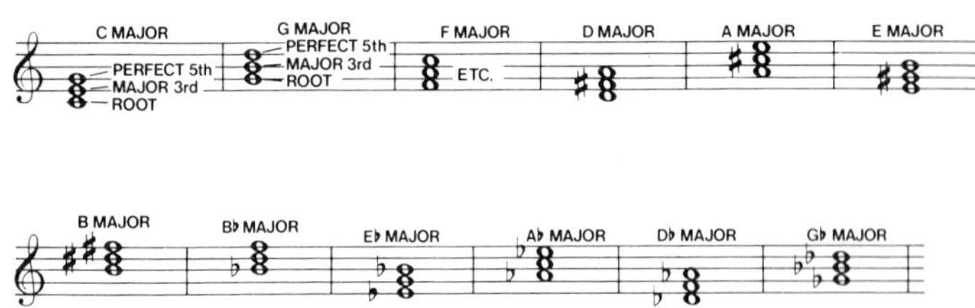

(NB I am assuming you know by now that F♯ major sounds the same as G♭ major, and am therefore not writing out all the alternative versions.)

If we use a minor 3rd instead of a major 3rd, and keep the other two notes the same, the chord becomes a *minor chord.* PERFECT 5th MINOR 3rd ROOT C MINOR

In sheet music, chords are often written in a sort of shorthand; a major chord will be written simply as C, G, D or whatever. (It is not necessary to write in the 'major'). Minor chords are written Cm, Gm, Dm, etc.

To acquaint you with these symbols, here are a few random major and minor chords in various keys and positions:

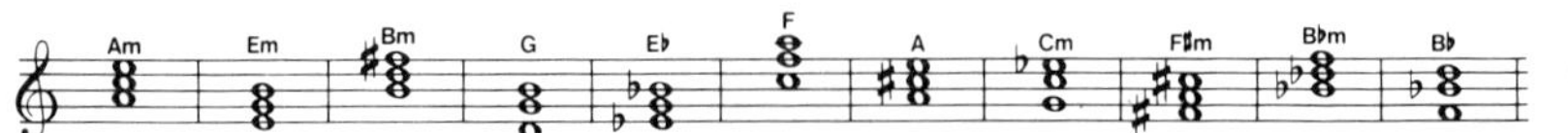

For obvious reasons, scales and chords tend to work very closely together. If a melody is in the scale of C major, then a C major chord is an obvious choice for something that will harmonise with it; a G♯ minor chord *won't* sound so harmonious in conjunction with the C major scale. If, in a melody in the key of C major a long note of E occurred, then a C major chord would fit well underneath. A long F note would need a change of chord, unless that special 'suspended' effect of an F note over a C major chord was required; Dm or F would work fine.

There are *no rules* here, though. I am not writing this book to try to teach you how to compose music, or tell you whether it is permissible or not to use certain notes in conjunction with certain chords. You can use any note you like sounded against any chord. If you are clever, you'll even be able to make it sound good. I'm simply pointing out certain conventions which apply to diatonic (= in a key) music, to help you make sense of writing and reading it.

One problem that often occurs is knowing which chords to use to accompany a melody. If you know all the major or minor chords (and remember, there are only 24!) you are actually in a position to accompany most straightforward tunes, albeit in a clumsy and extremely boring way. But if more subtlety is required, our quest for extra chords must continue.

7th Chords

One of the simpler 4-note chords is the 7th (sometimes written *dominant* 7th). C7

Dominant is Latin for 'leading', and the dominant 7th chord does have a very strong feeling of wanting to lead to another chord. In fact it leads to another chord a 4th up, eg C7 to F or G7 to C, in such splendid and unequivocal style that experts on harmony have dubbed this chordal movement a *Perfect Cadence*. Perfect it may well be but it is also astonishingly corny, having been over-used in popular music for the last hundred years.

Here are the twelve 7th chords in their most mundane positions:

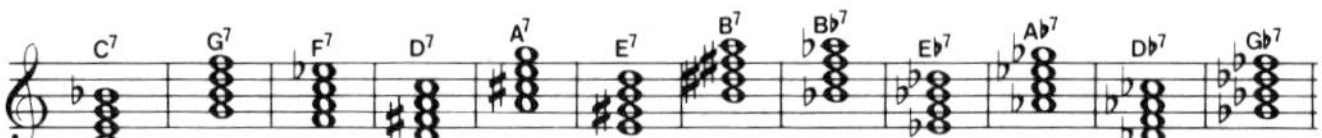

Now, there is a point here which could, quite easily, utterly confuse you.

The interval between (C) and (B♭) is, as you know, a minor 7th;

however when we describe a chord of

we refer to it as C7, not C minor 7. C minor 7 does exist, though. However, as in ordinary 3-note chords, the minor refers to the *3rd.* The chord of

C minor 7 is: 7th 5th MINOR 3rd ROOT

The important thing to remember when bandying about terms like *minor 7th* and *major 9th* is whether you are describing an interval or a chord. The same phrase can mean something quite different, as we have already seen.

Minor 7th chords are much nicer than ordinary 7th chords. I shan't bother writing them all out in each key, but do remember that in any one key a minor 7th (or indeed, any other) chord can be played lots of different ways. All these chords are variants of A minor 7:

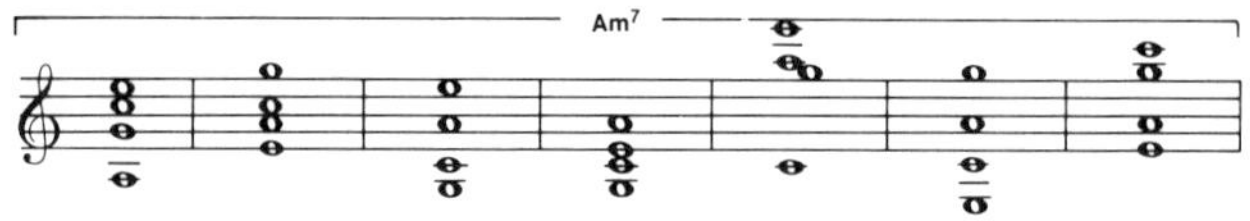

Due to the limitations of the guitar, some of these would not be playable on the instrument, but here are a few which are:

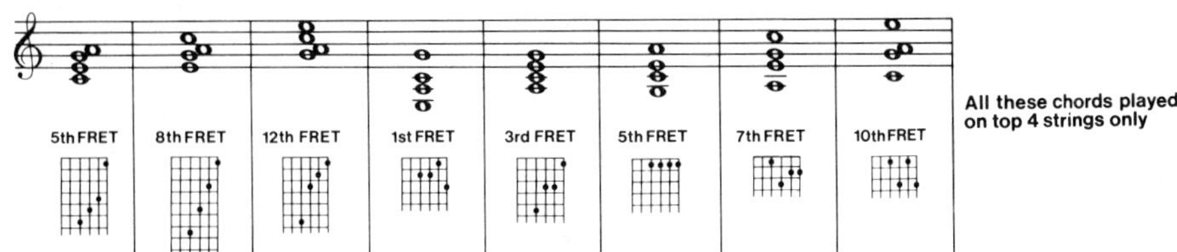

In any case, I am not so much concerned with exactly what can or cannot be played on various instruments, more with the idea of chord voicings in the abstract. After all, chords are not confined to what just one person can play; they can be made up by a combination of different instruments (for example, a 4-note chord produced by oboe, clarinet, bassoon and French horn each playing one note). Or, in a rock band, one guitarist could play one chord while the keyboard player simultaneously played another, thereby producing an interesting composite chord. While it is true that there are certain pianistic chords (notably ones with big intervals or lots of 'clusters')

ie: 

which cannot be played on guitar, there are some beautiful, subtle voicings of guitar chords which a piano cannot duplicate. Basically, a chord voiced in a certain way will have a certain musical character or effect, and it is as well to be familiar with those effects, whatever instrument you play.

Answers to 'Spot The Interval' quiz

1 Perfect 5th; 2 Major 6th; 3 Major 3rd; 4 Octave; 5 Diminished 5th; 6 Minor 6th; 7 Minor 7th; 8 Octave; 9 Minor 3rd; 10 Augmented 4th; 11 Minor 6th; 12 Major 7th; 13 Perfect 5th; 14 Minor 7th; 15 Perfect 4th; 16 Perfect 4th; 17 Perfect 5th; 18 Minor 3rd; 19 Major 6th; 20 Octave; 21 Octave & Major 6th.

7 Chords II

As chords and chord voicings are something of a favourite subject of mine, I would like to stay with them for the next few chapters. Let us refer back to ordinary major chords for the moment. These, the simplest of chords, are the simplest to voice, but even these three notes can be arranged in a number of different ways. For a keyboard player in a modern beating group, the obvious task will be to play the chord with one hand, leaving the other free to dramatically punch the air, to turn amp volume controls up to '10', and to lash the roadies with knotted mic leads (goes down a storm in the States). Therefore we arrive at these three time-honoured voicings of

C major: 

Clever geezers like myself can also manage C MAJOR C MAJOR

and sometimes C MAJOR if I've had enough to drink, and most players will

get round to putting in extra notes on the first three: C MAJOR C MAJOR C MAJOR

Which is best? Well, only you can be the judge of that; there are no rules on the subject. Listen to the various voicings available and decide which sounds best to you, but bear in mind that *context* may change this.

To take an example; you might be given a chord sequence for a song the verse of which is depicted as follows:

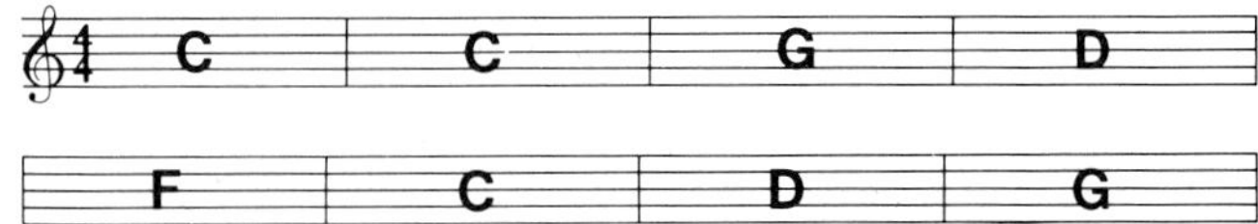

(Remembering that C, F, etc are abbreviations for the chords of C major and F major.) If you try to play this 'progression' sticking rigidly to one voicing or chord-shape:

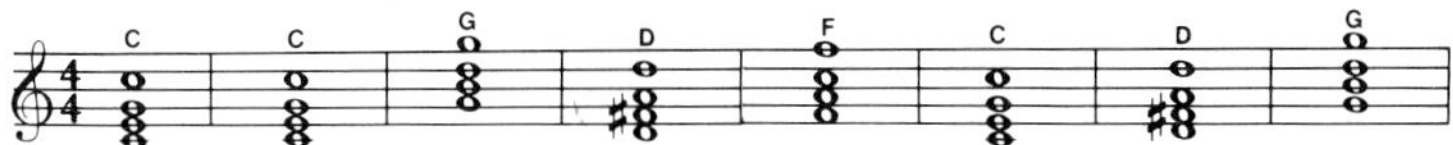

it will tend to sound a bit stiff. If, however, you have the ability to utilise different shapes, the results will sound more fluid:

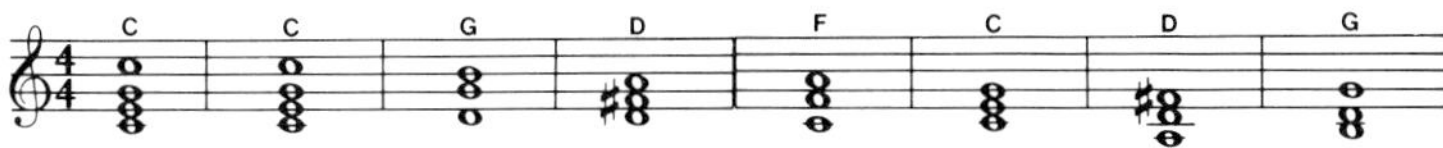

(It's not a great sequence anyway, but never mind!)

So even with straight major chords played with one hand only, a keyboard player has a huge range of choice over voicings; a guitarist has it too, though the possibilities may be a little harder to see initially. The careful exercise of this choice is what can help make a very good musician out of an ordinary one, as chords are all-important in music; a good player will usually be the one who really knows chords and voicings, and who knows what scales can be used in conjunction with them. By the way, everything I have said about major chords applies also to minor chords—the three 'ingredients' are the same (root, third and fifth) except that the third is a minor third, not a major; the three notes can be played in as many combinations.

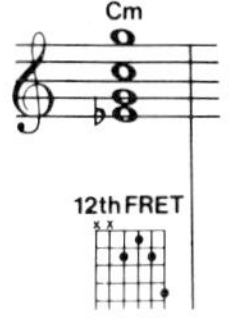

is a nice voicing of a minor chord.

6th Chords

Adding an extra note to a chord expands the choice of voicings by a vast degree. (By extra note I do not mean adding another E to a C major chord, but bringing in a new element like an A or B to make up a C6 or C7 chord.) The possibilities are greater and so the choice has to be exercised that much more carefully. Great fun it is, too! Here are some different

voicings of C6: 

An interesting ambiguity crops up here. Look at the first three C6 chords —aren't they exactly the same as the first three examples of A minor 7 guitar chords?

Well, in fact, they are, and this gives rise to the interesting problem wherein the same combination of 4 notes can be called either Am7 or C6. An A, C, E and G can either be seen as (respectively) the root, minor 3rd,

perfect 5th and minor 7th of an Am7 chord:

Am7
MINOR 7th
PERFECT 5th
MINOR 3rd
ROOT

or the major 6th,

root, major 3rd and perfect 5th of a C6 chord:

C6
PERFECT 5th
MAJOR 3rd
ROOT
MAJOR 6th

This is a little confusing, a good example of the all-pervading ambiguity of music; there are after all only 12 available notes, so they often have to do more than one job! On paper then, the chord is the same—but the question of which way you *hear* it is very interesting indeed. What tends to happen is that the context in which the chord is placed and (more important) the *bass note* played underneath it would determine which of the two it sounded like. If you heard the chord in conjunction with a low bass note of C, you would hear it as C6; if the chord was then repeated but with the bass note changed to A you would hear it as an Am7.

The 'bass note' factor does in fact throw everything into a different light. A chord in itself might have a certain sound which suggests 'majorness', but in conjunction with a different bass note it can suggest 'minorness'. The chord itself has not changed, only its musical setting. I'll give more examples of this as we progress.

More chords; you should now know about major and minor chords, and you've seen a few examples of 6th chords (sometimes referred to as *added 6th*). A further combination is of course the minor 6th chord; this is an ordinary minor chord (root/minor 3rd/perfect 5th) with the sixth note of the scale added. Now the *6th* chord, if one were in an uncharitable mood, could be deemed the greasiest chord in the whole of popular music. Voiced

in this particularly unacceptable fashion

the 'added 6th' is always used as the final chord of such master works as *Edelweiss* and *Those Lazy, Hazy, Crazy Days of Summer* as if to prove in one cheap flourish how *socially acceptable* and *normal* those tunes are. Whereas the *major* 6th has a blandly triumphant, conclusively cabaret ring to it and is thus ideally suited to bringing geriatric melodies to a falsely encouraging halt, its brother the *minor* 6th is maudlin and pathetic, often cruelly misused as accompaniment to blubbering wretches singing of distant and unavailable sweethearts 'many moiles away in dear ould Dublin town'. If you persist in being interested in minor 6ths, consider these voicings at your own peril:

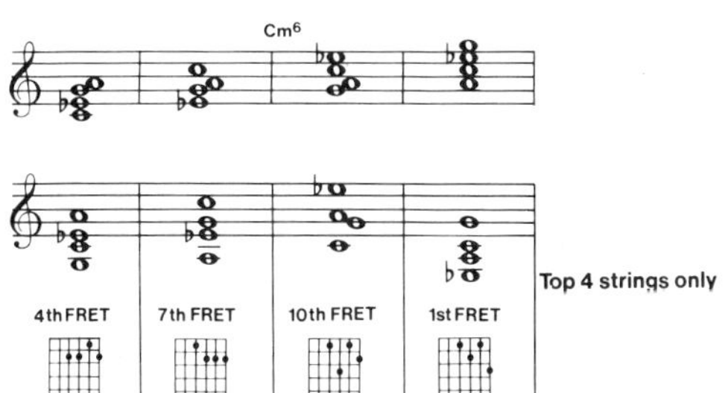

but don't blame me if elderly relatives burst into tear-stained melodic reminiscence while you're practising.

8 Chords III

Having dealt with major and minor chords, 6th chords and 7th chords, it would be wise to consider two more permutations.

Diminished and Augmented Chords
A diminished chord starts off much the same as a minor chord, but goes mad halfway up. C minor is: PERFECT FIFTH MINOR THIRD ROOT

whereas C diminished (written *C dim* or sometimes *C°*) looks like this: MAJOR SIXTH DIMINISHED FIFTH MINOR THIRD ROOT

It is the diminished fifth interval within the chord that gives it its name. If you examine the diminished chord carefully, you will see that it is made up of three equal intervals; C to E♭, E♭ to G♭ and G♭ to A, all minor thirds.

A fifth note added to these four would be a C octave: , and the interval between that and the A below it is again a minor 3rd.

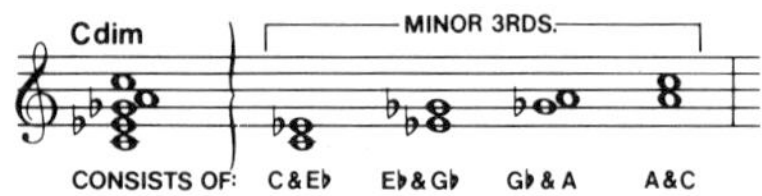

This has an interesting implication; as diminished chords are always made up of successions of minor third intervals, the same four notes will

serve to make up four different chords. In other words is C dim; is E♭ dim, but the same four notes are in use. Similarly, G♭ dim is and A dim is although the notes are positioned differently on the stave, C, E♭, G♭ and A are common to all four chords and the chords are thus essentially the same. A further implication is that there are, therefore, only three different types of diminished chord.

The first contains the notes C, E♭, G♭ and A and is C dim, E♭ dim, G♭ dim or A dim.

The second contains the notes C♯, E, G, and B♭ and is C♯ dim, E dim, G dim or B♭ dim.

The third contains the notes D, F, A♭ and B and is D dim, F dim, A♭ dim or B dim.

The musical effect of a diminished chord (characterised by a feeling of mild suspense) is such that whatever the voicing, the chord sounds very similar; this is because the intervals acting within the chord are equal. Any diminished chord is thus interchangeable between four keys.

One finds that the augmented chord is subject to the same sort of mad logic. To arrive at an augmented chord, we take an ordinary major chord (once again, C will do).

and sharpen or *augment* the fifth.
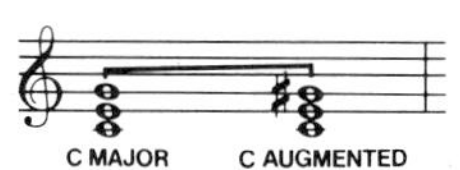

The interval between C and G♯ is known as an *augmented 5th* (as the less dull-witted of you will recall) and this interval gives the augmented chord its name.

Like the diminished chord, the augmented chord is made up of equal intervals—in this case, the interval is a *major* third. C and E, E and G♯, and G♯ and C are all major thirds, so the same three notes can serve as three different chords. C augmented (usually abbreviated to *C aug*) is

E aug is: and G♯ aug is:

Different voicings, same three notes. There are then only four possible types of augmented chord.

The first contains the notes C, E and G♯, and is C aug, E aug or G♯ aug.

The second contains the notes D♭, F, and A, and is D♭ aug, F aug or A aug.

The third contains the notes D, F♯ and A♯, and is D aug, F♯ aug or A♯ aug.

And the fourth contains the notes E♭, G, and B, and is E♭ aug, G aug or B aug.
(One great advantage of this of course is that, unlike other chords, you need not learn diminished and augmented chords in all twelve keys!)

Note at this point that there are no minor or major variations of diminished and augmented chords. In a way they are in a class of their own; whereas a sixth chord might be either a major sixth or a minor sixth, a diminished chord is simply *diminished!* You could in fact regard the diminished chord (consisting as it does entirely of minor 3rd intervals) as a special sort of minor chord, and by the same reasoning an augmented chord could be seen as a kind of major chord, as it is all made up of major 3rds.

Please remember that it is the *third* of a chord which determines whether the chord is minor or major.

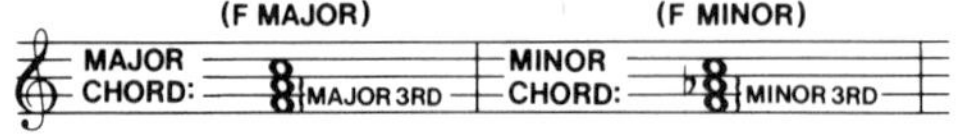

If you are in any doubt about this, count the semitones between the root and the third; a minor third is three semitones up from the root, whereas the major third is four semitones up. (For guitarists—a minor third is three frets up from the root, the major third is four frets up.) Better still try to get used to the difference in sound; of the two, the major has a brighter ring to it:

while the minor sounds a bit sad:

On chord charts, major chords such as C major, G♯ major and B♭ major will usually be abbreviated to plain C, G♯, and B♭, and minor chords are written C m, G♯ m, and B♭ m (etc).

We're now going to take a quick sidelong glance at:

9th Chords

To some of you the words 'ninth chord' may evoke agonising guitar shapes like

playable only after plastic surgery and sounding suspiciously like (dare I say it) jazz. May I suggest that you rough types amuse yourselves by defacing the rest of this book with your crucifixes while the rest of us sip our rare liqueurs and, settling back into sumptuous red leather armchairs, discuss with all due solemnity the glorious ninth. ('Why I remember the time—'77 I think it was—*marvellous* concert, Soft Machine at Heidelburg town hall . . .' [murmurs of appreciation] '. . . some sort of bloody socialist do.

That oboist chappie, Jenkins, played a minor ninth chord for $3\frac{1}{2}$ hours. *Remarkable* endurance . . .' [etc].)

Having constructed a chord as far up as the seventh, the next logical extra note to add is the ninth, that is the note an octave and a tone above the root of the chord

1 2 3 4 5 6 7 8 9

This chord is C dominant 7, written C7, and this is C7/9:

The interval between (C) (the root) and (D) is a major ninth, and

any C chord containing a D note will be called some sort of ninth. 'Minor ninth' chords are arrived at by adding the ninth to a minor or minor

seventh chord: Cm7 Cm7/9

Here are a few different voicings of minor ninth chords which might appeal to you:

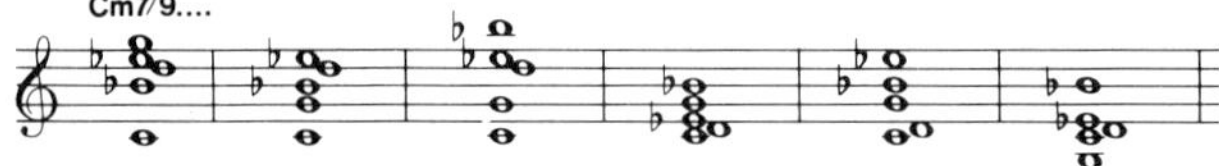

(Notice that in the latter three of these the ninth has been brought down an octave to sit in with the rest of the chord. Although the note is then technically a 'second' rather than a ninth, the chord is still a ninth chord!)

It is by no means obligatory to use the seventh in conjunction with the ninth:

C9

is an example where the seventh has been omitted altogether from the chord—the chord name is then correctly a C9 rather than a C7/9. These voicings

of ninth chords also omit the seventh, and still sound good . . . obviously, when this point of chord construction is reached, the number of elements involved (root, third, fifth, seventh and ninth) gives an enormous choice over voicings, and it can often be beneficial to omit a note in order that the chord might sound more 'open', or less cluttered.

9 Chords IV

And now, let me introduce you to the

Major 7th Chords
These are chords in which the seventh is major. In an ordinary dominant chord the seventh is at an interval of a *minor* seventh from the root of the chord. 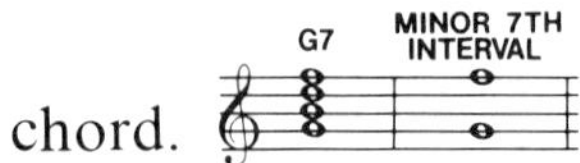

Though the chord itself is major (as determined by the third—the G and B interval of a major third means the chord has to be a major), the seventh is a minor seventh. In the *chord* of the minor 7th, both the third and the seventh are minor. 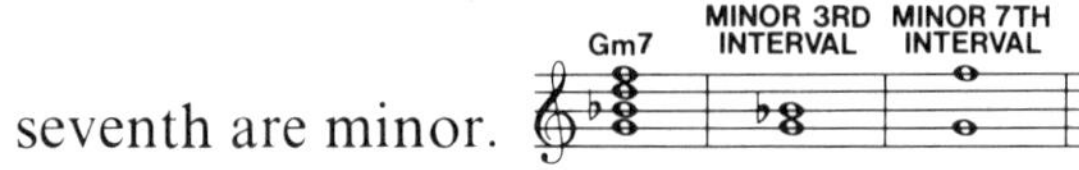

Now a major 7th chord is perhaps more natural as, unlike a dominant 7th, it employs as a seventh a note which occurs naturally in the major scale based on the root of the chord. The major scale of C is:

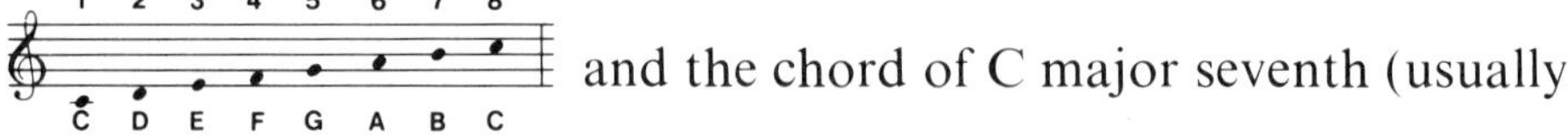

and the chord of C major seventh (usually abbreviated to Cmaj7) employs the seventh note of that scale. 

For the key of G the major seventh chord is formed by adding an F♯ to the major triad.

These are the major seventh chords for each key:

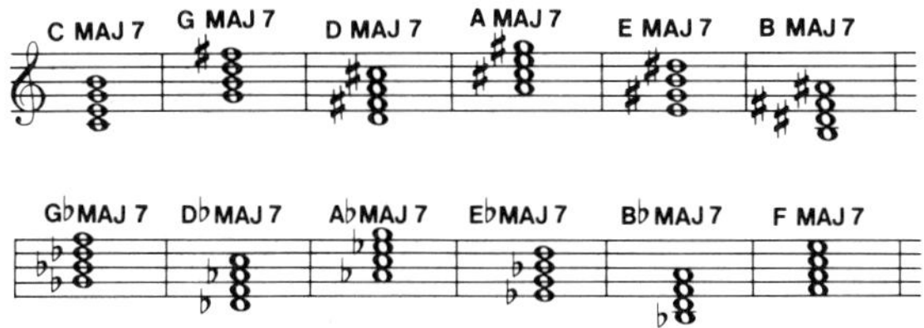

(You will notice that the major seventh is one semitone below the name note of the chord; the seventh is sometimes referred to as the *leading note*, as in melodic and scalic terms it leads to the note a semitone above it, the octave.)

The examples that I have given show the major seventh chord in its most basic voicing, with the seventh sitting neatly and symmetrically on top of the major triad. As you know, though, any chord can be voiced in a variety of different ways, and the major seventh is no exception. One simple alteration would be to bring the seventh down an octave, while leaving the major triad unmoved.

This actually sounds very good despite the slight dissonance of the interval within the chord. (*Dissonant* = jarring, clashing, discordant) . . . or, if you like, *because* of that slight dissonance, the voicing sounds more interesting than the

Chords often work in this sweet'n'sour way; this chord:

(another voicing of Cmaj7) contains the rather jarring dissonance of 

which, when played alone, sounds a bit gruesome. When the inner E and G are inserted, however, the chord sounds beautiful. At first the ear might tend to be offended by the (minor 9th) interval even when the other notes were present

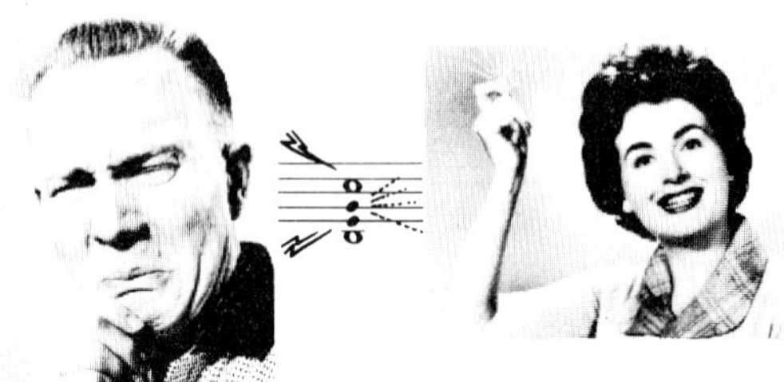

but like all good sensory experiences, the appreciation is an acquired taste. A bit like getting to enjoy the more pungent cheeses.

But I digress. Open your desks and take out your banjos and accordions. I am going to go out of the room for half an hour, and when I come back I want you all to have learnt these C major 7 voicings off by heart. You never know, you might even like some of them. You might even work them into a song, in which case my lawyer will be in touch with you immediately concerning copyright infringement and damages which I am prepared to waive in favour of my modest fee of 60% of all royalties . . .

C MAJOR 7.....

7 12 12 3 10 5 1 8

Inversions and Alternative Bass Notes

I am aware that any bassists or drummers reading this might be getting a little fidgety about the lack of rhythm-section orientated info. For the former, then, this section—and for the latter, a forthcoming chapter positively brimming with paradiddles.

In my opinion, British bassists have for far too long got away with thundering out indistinct but vaguely reassuring root notes underneath the chords painstakingly created by their more sensitive guitarist and keyboard colleagues. The time has come for them to leave their vantage point at the artists' bar and weigh in with some harmonic groundwork.

Take this chord sequence:

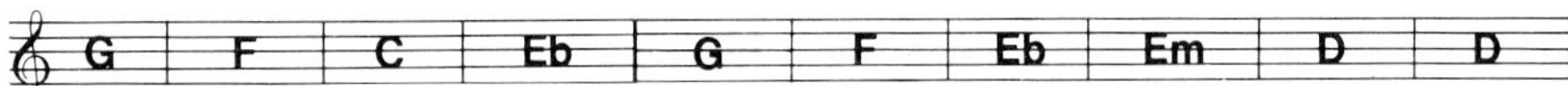

Obviously, a bass player can get by, simply by booming out the roots to each chord, but a different choice of bass notes could make the sequence sound more interesting:

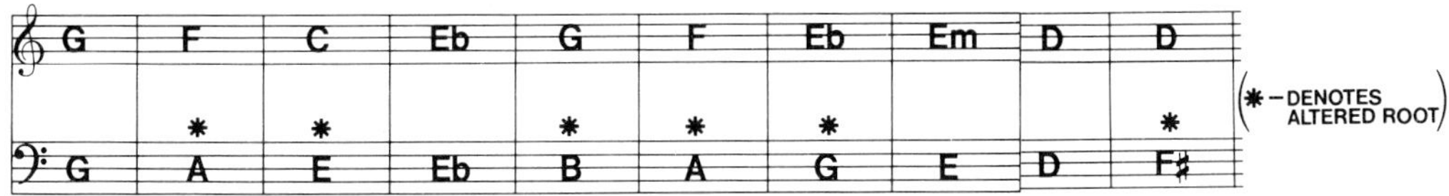

Playing bass in this style creates *inversions* to the chords. If the bass plays the third of the chord instead of the root, the chord is said to be a '1st inversion'—take the second chord in the sequence above, an F major chord with an A bass note; this is called F 1st inversion, written F ①. (The minor version would be F minor with an A♭ bass note—this is Fm 1st inversion, or Fm ①.)

If the bass plays the fifth of a chord, it is called a '2nd inversion'. G major with a D bass note is called G 2nd inversion, written G ②, and the minor version of that is Gm ②. All quite simple if you know your triads! Occasionally 3rd inversions crop up, which is when the bass daringly plays the seventh of a seventh chord: C7 with a B♭ bass note is called C7 3rd inversion (written C7③ and C major 7 with a B bass note is Cmaj7③. Looking back over the sequence with the altered bass notes, you can see that I have made chords 2, 3, 5, 6, 7 and 10 into 1st inversions by having the bass play the third of the chord.

Apart from the three inversions, it is possible for the bass to play other 'altered' root notes to interesting effect. Let us, once again, take C major as our example.

We know the notes of C, E and G will work in the bass:

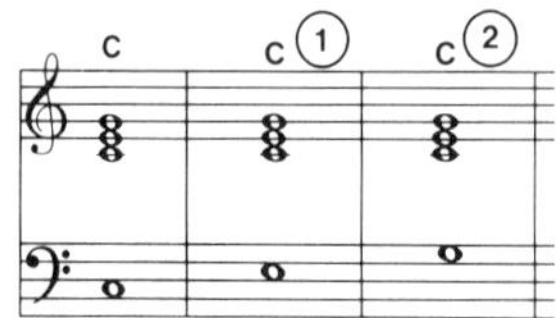

(They have to, really, as they are all notes contained in the chord already!) A 'B' bass note gives us a Cmaj7③ and if the B is flattened to a B♭ we arrive at a C7 ③. These last two often occur when descending bass lines are used:

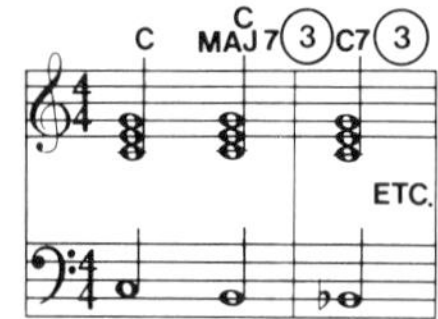

What happens if we go on descending to an 'A' note? At this point, as I have mentioned before, the C major chord changes its identity and becomes an Am7 chord.

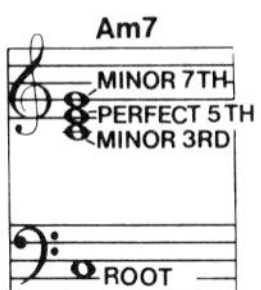

You could argue that in theory it is still a C chord with a sixth (A) in the bass, but in practice it *sounds* like an Am chord—try it and see!

If I might be permitted to extend this idea to its obvious conclusion, you could also try playing 'F' and 'D' bass notes under a C major chord. An 'F' sounds really good, giving this chord

(which I personally would describe as 'C over F bass', though it could be regarded as an Fmaj7/9 (no 3rd) . . . think about it!). I like this chord a lot, and quite often change the root of a major chord up a fourth (or down a fifth) in my own music. A 'D' note does not sound quite so good initially

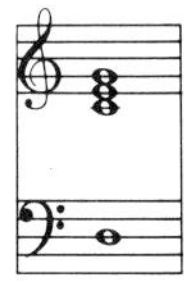

(but a subtle improvement is to add a major seventh to the chord thus

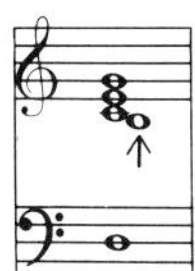

which improves the effect. (Actually this last chord could be seen as a type of 'D13' chord, but as we haven't got that far with chords we had better not dwell on it!)

So you can see that it is possible to use any note from the C major scale (C, D, E, F, G, A and B) as a bass note to a C major chord. I am *not* suggesting that it is desirable for the bassist *always* to alter the root, merely that alternatives exist. Keyboard players, due to the clear layout of their instruments, are in a better position to spot these alternatives (which is why keyboard players often end up as arrangers) but guitarists and bassists should be aware of them. All I am saying really is that in order for someone to improvise well, they *must* be aware of what notes will work with which chords and be prepared to play some of the less obvious ones. In the right context, a bassist playing inversions and alternative root notes is a joy to hear, as it brings the bass into its rightful category as a musical instrument capable of melodic and harmonic contributions as well as rhythmic ones.

10 Drum Notation

My self-imposed career as a musical aesthete has led me several times to seek employment in low-life haunts. Though one hastens to draw a veil over what goes on backstage at *Let My People Come* (a West End musical sex comedy) I can reveal that it was there that I first met Bob Emmines, who was playing drums in the show. Nightly, the band (I name no names) would assemble to grind out ghastly show tunes while luridly-lit buttocks weaved in front of their faces . . . however, Bob seems to have survived this enriching experience sufficiently to explain to me the rudiments of drum notation, and these I now pass on to you.

Although kit drums (as opposed to tympani and the like) do not produce actual tuned notes, drum parts are written on a musical stave, the bass stave:

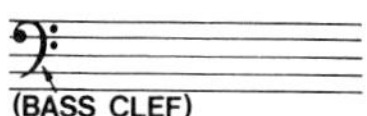

Each part of the kit has its own part of the stave; snare drum parts are written on the 2nd space down (ie on the space which would normally be E):

Bass drum is written on the bottom space:

Tom toms are written in the spaces either side of the snare; small toms take the higher space and floor toms the lower:

(As this system of notation was formalised at a time when two tom toms was the norm, a special system has to be used to notate parts for kits comprising lots of tom toms. I'll come to this in a while.)

Thus, you can see that the drums are arranged across the stave with the 'highs' (small tom tom and snare drum) at the top and the 'lows' (floor tom tom and bass drum) at the bottom. An extremely simple drum part might look like this:

The symbol at the end is probably worrying you—permit me to elucidate . . . it is an accented crash cymbal note, which sounds like this:

(The little sign above the note (>) is an *accent* sign, meaning 'hit it a bit harder'.)

Cymbal parts are written resting on the top line of the stave. Their rhythm is denoted by small crosses rather than ordinary notation, which serves to differentiate them from drum parts—this can be a great help when a part is very busy as it offers the eye a contrasting feature. Here are the cymbal notes written alongside their equivalent in normal notation:

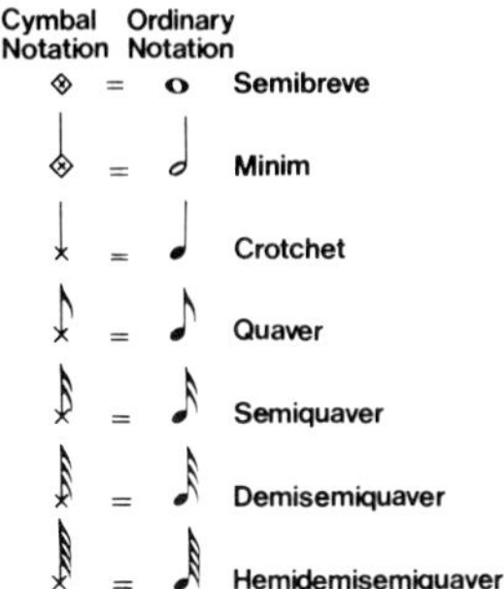

Hi-hat parts (if the hi-hat is played with a stick) are written on the same space as the other cymbals:

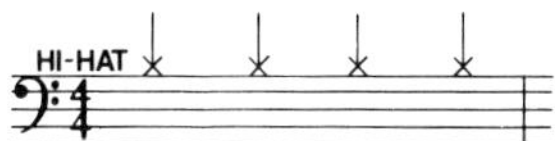

As the same line therefore serves for crash, ride and hi-hat cymbals, it is necessary to specify which one is to be played. If more than one cymbal is to be played simultaneously, leger lines can be used to create an extra space above the first cymbal space:

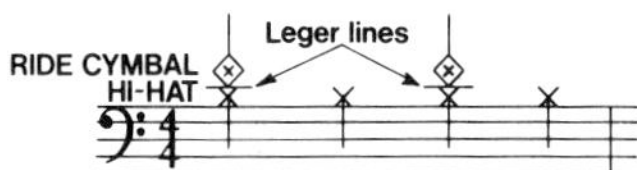

As a general rule then, the whole drum kit is written across the bass stave with high sounds at the top and low sounds at the bottom. The only exception to this rule is that when the hi-hat is pedalled, rather than struck with a stick, it is written down on the bottom space with the bass drum:

If, on some beats, the two are played simultaneously, the cross indicating the hi-hat beat sits on the stem of the bass drum note:

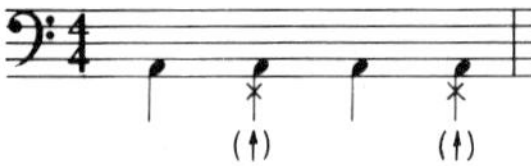

Open or shut hi-hat can be indicated by means of writing noughts or crosses above the notes, eg:

(Obviously, this can only apply when the hi-hat is sticked.)

When lots of tom toms are employed, the parts can be written across two linked staves:

so that a multiple tom tom break could be written:

The exact positioning of each drum on the stave then depends on the number of toms in use. A simple instruction to 'run round the kit' might be simpler here, but tireless wags such as Bob Emmines have been known to leap up, tear round the front of their kit, and crash back on to their stools when confronted with such a command. (You *need* a sense of humour to play in *Let My People Come* every night for two years.)

Personally, I think it is a real bore for the drummer to be told exactly what to do in drum breaks, because it destroys all spontaneity and negates the possibility of using imagination. How would you like to sit there for hours going '*boum kaf boum kaf*' waiting patiently for the opportunity to lash out with a '*phlakaton phlakaton raka-taka boum bediddley BISH*' only to be told on arriving at the 128th bar that the arranger had a '*dugga dugga dugga dugga ping*' in mind? However, there are plenty of arrangers around who think they know best, and people planning hit singles do not like to leave anything to chance.

Most drummers that I know actually use notation as a rough guide only. They will have a sketch of the structure of the piece, eg:

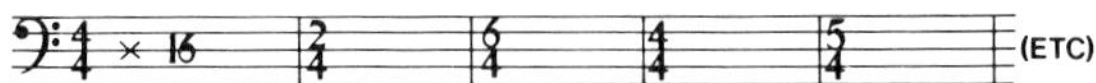

and then will write in accents wherever relevant:

This means that they are then free to play in their own style throughout the piece while knowing where they are on the chart. The great advantage that 'reading' drummers have over non-readers is an ability to run mentally through a piece just by looking through a written part; this saves the rest of the group having to play the number 35 times at a rehearsal till the drummer 'gets it' (by which time the rest of the group will be sick of playing the piece and the finance company will have repossessed all the equipment).

Also, a drummer who can write music will be able to jot down interesting little rhythmic patterns etc that need to be remembered, and be able to refer to them at any time without all the paraphernalia of tape recorders.

A couple more small points about drum notation. The only way a drummer can sustain a 'note' on an ordinary drum is to play a roll. If a note lasting a whole $\frac{4}{4}$ bar was required, it would be written:

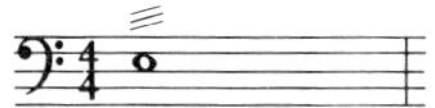

which is actually shorthand for:

In classical percussion notation (say, for example, an orchestral snare drum part) the same thing would be written:

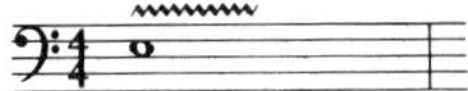

Cowbell parts are written with small diamonds, ie:

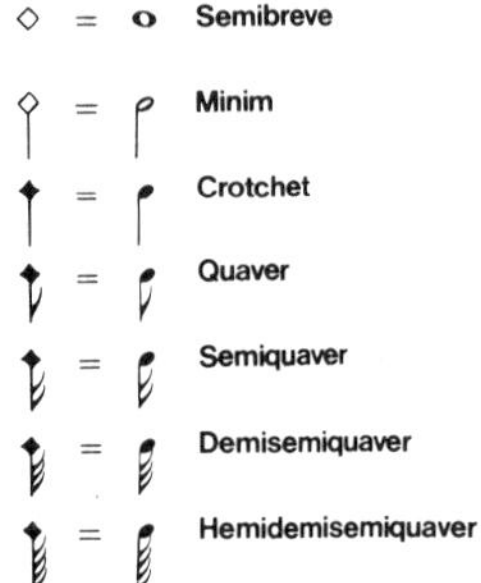

Parts for cowbells are written on the cymbal space. The more alert among you will be protesting that, even at a fast tempo, a cowbell note could not possibly last as long as a whole bar . . . well, I've got news for you: you are absolutely right. But it might occur occasionally as a *rolled* note:

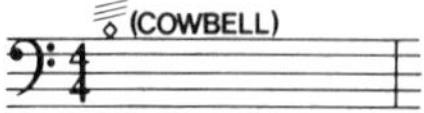

even though one shudders to think of the musical effect. Kindly add the 'rolled cowbell semibreve' to your growing list of impressive-sounding musical rarities, along with the Hemidemisemiquaver and the Double Flat (3 room k & b, no pets). Then, when the existence of such things is challenged or smirked at by some doubting anti-technicalist, you can point out (in a voice oozing with smug satisfaction), 'Ah, but you know dear boy, they *do* exist.'

11 Writing it Down I

When *Sound International* first rashly asked me to do the series of articles which I have incorporated into this book, my brief was to 'write something about reading and writing music'. So far I have written a fair bit about reading music and the symbols involved, but nothing about actually *writing* it. This is, I suspect, a stumbling block for a lot of musicians. The idea of taking a pen and making marks on a piece of paper seems to have little to do with playing music, especially rock music. But as I have said before, this facility can be helpful in so many ways; firstly, it is an aid to memory—sure, you can remember how to play a song without writing it down, but for how long?

Also, the ability to write something down is an aid to communication. It means you can demonstrate music to another musician without actually having to play it!

But there remains a block against actually writing music down. One reason for this, I think, is that we only tend to see notated music in this form:

This bit of music has, in fact, been prepared by an artist, using 'Letraset' symbols, special pens, rulers etc, and it probably took him 10 minutes to do. All the diagrams you have seen in this book have been specially drawn by the same artist and for the sake of clearness and legibility he has taken his time in preparing each one. The trouble is, that same clearness and legibility can seem a little imposing. You might think, 'I can't write music as neatly as that. Mine comes out looking all messy and silly!' You might be surprised to learn that when I do the initial rough diagrams that the artist tarts up, they look like this:

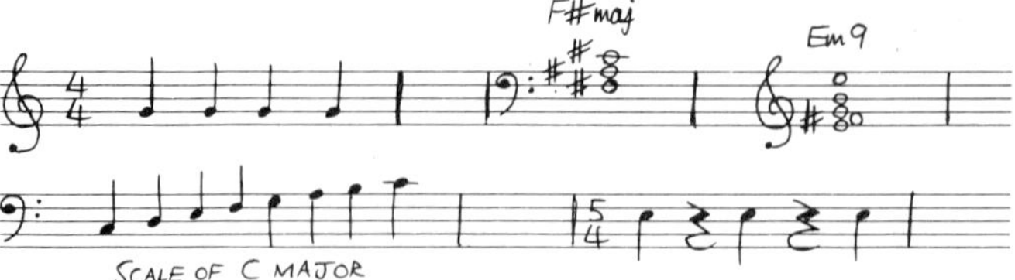

(etc). I can knock out about 15 of these in five minutes, and it does not bother me that they are a bit imperfect-looking, because they are still legible.

The point is, when you write in your ordinary handwriting

Dear Aunt Dorothy

Thank you ever so much for the particle accelerator and thermonuclear devices.

you don't worry that it doesn't look like

Dear Aunt Dorothy,
Thank you ever so much for the particle accelerator and thermonuclear devices.

or

Dear Aunt Dorothy,
Thank you ever so much for the particle accelerator and thermonuclear devices.

Similarly in music writing, you should aim for a style that *you* can read and understand, and never mind if it looks a bit informal. Here is how to get started.

The first thing to worry about is the stave on which the notes are written. You can buy stuff called *manuscript paper* from music shops which comes with blank staves, like this:

There are quite a few different types, the chief variant being the number of staves per sheet; I've found that '10 stave' (10 staves per sheet) is the best for most things as it leaves room between the staves for writing in lyrics, chord symbols, etc.

If you are really poor you could draw the staves yourself, but unless you are good at geometry they come out looking like this:

(A friend of mine has a special five-pointed nib for drawing staves, but they are fairly scarce.)

Having got the manuscript paper, do not be intimidated by its creamy virgin whiteness. Mess up a couple of sheets—get a few pens and pencils and try drawing a few musical symbols

(𝅗𝅥 ♩ ♪ ♬ ♯ ♭ etc)

to get the feel. Some pens are better than others for music writing—felt tips are OK, unless they bleed through to the other side. Some ballpoints are duff because they make little blotches; fountain pens can be good if you get the right one. I (spot the professional) sometimes using a Rotring *Rapidograph*, a pen developed for technical drawing. This gives a very even

line which is good for 'note stems', these things  , and has a variety

of different nib sizes, mine being a 0·5. Although this pen is really neat, it's slow and sometimes a bit scratchy, so I generally use a felt tip with a small point or a ballpoint; the main thing is to find a pen with which *you* feel comfortable.

Now, what do you want to write down? What do you mean, you don't know? There must be *some* little piece that you play (even if it is only a 5-note riff) that you would like to immortalise. If you are a singer or guitarist and want to write down a melody line, the first thing to draw on

the stave is the treble clef:

This is quite difficult, a lot of people give up at this point. If it is any

consolation, my one looks like this:

A pretty sorry specimen, eh? Recognisable, though, and that is all it has to be. By the way, the final line of the treble clef traditionally ends up touching

the 'G' line of the stave

and in olden days the clef was called the 'G clef' . . . This is one of the musical symbols you might need to practise drawing, as it is a bit of a beast to get right at first. Don't worry if your attempts come out a bit

deformed at first:

You should now work out what the notes in your melody are, for which purpose you might find useful the diagrams at the end of chapter 2. Here are two reminders for those of you too impatient to keep turning back the pages:

1 The open top 'E' string of the guitar is written:

and the other five open strings are written: 

2 Middle C (that is the C nearest the lock on your piano lid!)

is written:

Vocal parts and guitar parts both *sound* an octave lower than written, so the note when written for guitar or man's voice actually sounds

(The exception to this is of course the Bee Gees, who, given a note

will sing .)

I will assume, then, that you *can* work out the notes and where they should go on the stave. A good plan now is to make a preliminary rough sketch of your tune by simply writing out the notes in order, without bar lines.

As a further guide, lyrics should be written in underneath the notes if the tune is a vocal one.

Technically speaking, the next consideration should be the key signature, as that is always written first in a piece of music, but that can be deferred until the rhythm of the notes has been investigated.

So, the first question is, what is the time signature? Try tapping your foot while playing or humming the tune. If the pattern of leg movement that emerges is the repetitive, never-changing disco thump, it is extremely likely that your tune is in $\frac{4}{4}$. (Congratulations! You may have a hit on your hands.) If it is a *ONE*-two-three *ONE*-two-three beat as in EDELWEISS, THE LAST WALTZ or GOD SAVE THE QUEEN (how I love those tunes) it is in $\frac{3}{4}$ (three crotchets per bar). If it is a fast shuffle (you know—dum der dum der dum der dum, what my friend guitarist Steve Hillage calls 'maypole music') then it is in $\frac{12}{8}$ or $\frac{6}{8}$. Obviously $\frac{6}{8}$ has the same relationship to $\frac{12}{8}$ as $\frac{2}{4}$ does to $\frac{4}{4}$; in most instances, the shorter measures ($\frac{6}{8}$, $\frac{2}{4}$) are avoided as they utilise twice as many bar lines. A slow blues like *Feel like I've done gone fixin' to dust my shower unit* by Blind Lemon Braithwaite will usually be written in a slow $\frac{12}{8}$ metre. There is often some debate over how 'dum der dum der dum der dum' should be written as it can be equally well represented by

or

Also, in many jazz 'swing' charts, what is actually $\frac{12}{8}$ will be written as $\frac{4}{4}$:

rather than

The rule of thumb as to what is best is simply to use whichever metre utilises the least amount of symbols per bar—fewer symbols are less trouble to write and easier to read!

. . . course, *your* tune's probably in $\frac{13}{8}$ or $\frac{5}{4}$ or some clever dick metre like that, but then you'd know that already. If in any doubt, consult a knowall like myself. Keep an eye open for parts of your tune where the normal time signature changes temporarily; it is quite common for a $\frac{4}{4}$ piece to have the odd bar of $\frac{2}{4}$, $\frac{3}{4}$, $\frac{5}{4}$ etc, normally in order to accommodate an asymmetric lyric or an errant drum fill . . . '*Like I have to hit all 7 tom toms man, so it'll have to be a* $\frac{7}{4}$ *bar!*'

12 Writing it Down II

Once you have decided what the right time signature for your tune is, you can write it in next to your treble clef:

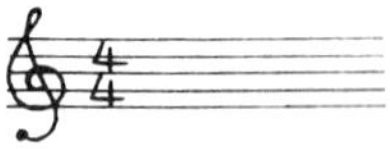

Having written it once you need not write it again, as it applies throughout the whole tune, unless contra-indicated by some new instruction. Now you have to work out how your sequence of notes fits into bars of $\frac{4}{4}$. This requires mental co-ordination. (*Wassat?*—Black Sabbath fan, London.) You have to sing or play the tune while mentally counting 1-2-3-4, 1-2-3-4, etc. Take it a bar at a time; count out the four beats of the first bar while humming or playing the beginning of your melody. With any luck, some of the notes will fall *on the beat*. Let us say that the first note falls on the first beat . . . where does the second note come? On the second beat perhaps? How convenient. It therefore follows that the first note is a crotchet, which is one beat of a $\frac{4}{4}$ bar. Write it in:

Now you can consider the third note—once you've decided where that falls, you can determine how long the *2nd* note is. Let's say that the 3rd note comes on the fourth beat of the bar:

3rd NOTE
Ist NOTE
BEATS: 1 2 3 4

The 2nd note therefore has to be two beats long—in other words, a minim.

Write it in:

We have now completed three beats of a four-beat bar, and unless the 4th note comes between the 3rd note and the end of the bar, we can complete

the bar by writing in that 3rd note: and adding a bar

line: 

Do not make the mistake of drawing in the bar lines first, or you will get this sort of thing happening:

Write in the notes first, otherwise it's a bit like putting in all the punctuation marks before writing a sentence!

Next problem: unless you have a particularly troglodyte mentality, you'll find that not all the notes of your melody fall on the beat. For any note falling off the beat there are three main notational possibilities (which coincide with the three main ways of subdividing the beat!)

The first possibility is that it is a quaver off the beat. The beat

being (crotchets),

quaver off-beats fall thus:

You may test this in your tune by counting 1 and 2 and 3 and 4 and (etc). Any note falling on an 'and' is a quaver off the beat.

Secondly, one may further sub-divide the basic crotchet pulse into semiquavers, which may well accommodate your errant notes where quavers have failed. Try the following count: 1234 2234 3234 4234 (etc). Any note landing on these places

|1234 2234 3234 4234|

is a *semiquaver* off the beat. Circled arrows show notes falling a semiquaver after the beat, the others a semiquaver before the beat:

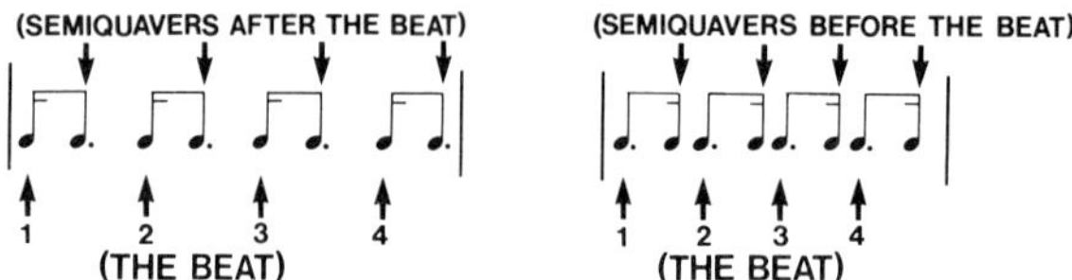

Now that all this is clear, you might well decide that in your melody the 1st note falls on the 1st beat, the 2nd note a semiquaver after the 2nd beat and the 3rd note a quaver after the 3rd beat. How to write this? Sub-divide the beat into semiquavers

and locate your three notes:

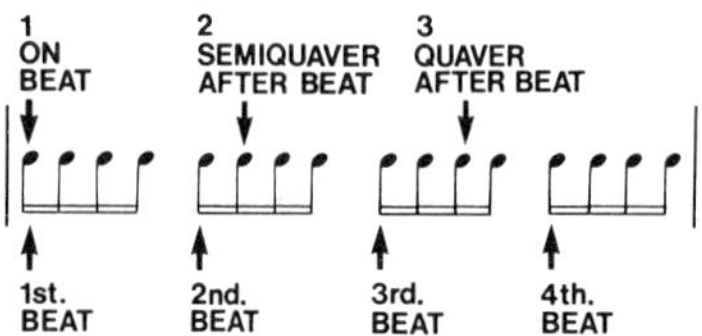

If no 4th note falls before the end of the bar, this can then be properly notated:

Note the use of ties here,

Fig 1 **Fig 2**

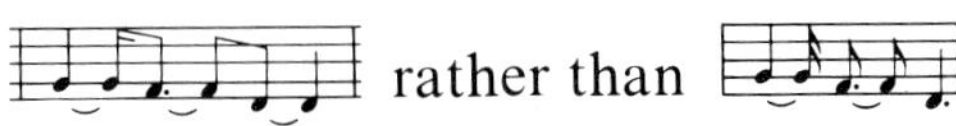
rather than

the ties enable us to see where the beat falls in relation to the played notes:

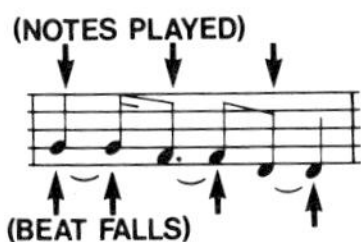
(NOTES PLAYED)
(BEAT FALLS)

The third main possibility for a note played off the beat is that it is part of a triplet grouping. (Those of you with a vestige of memory will remember that a triplet is a third division of the beat.) There are potentially as many different types of triplet as there are different note values, but these are the main three:

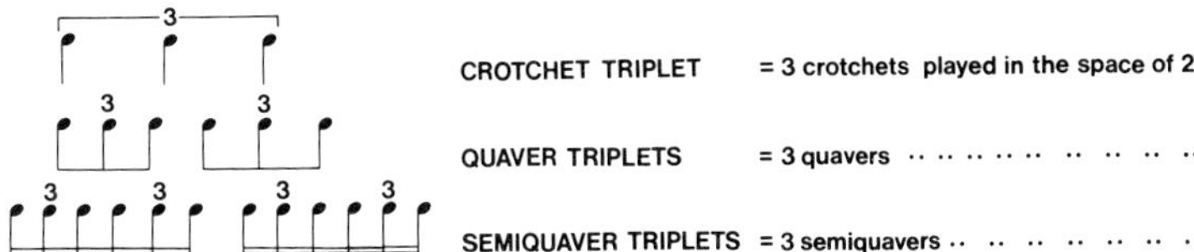
CROTCHET TRIPLET = 3 crotchets played in the space of 2
QUAVER TRIPLETS = 3 quavers .. ..
SEMIQUAVER TRIPLETS = 3 semiquavers .. ..

Occasionally a melody will feature a triplet, thus

and it can be quite difficult to distinguish

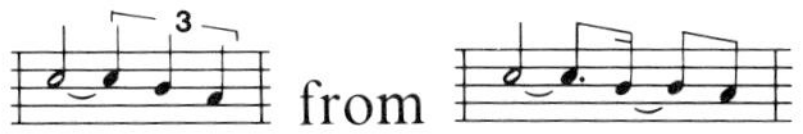
from

but trial and error and a bit of patience will in time enable you to make such distinctions confidently!

If the basic pulse of your tune is dotted crotchets rather than crotchets, notes played off the beat can be located by counting 123 223 323 423 (etc).

More often than not, you'll find off-beat accents located thus

and the commonest sort of 'dotted' configurations will involve a

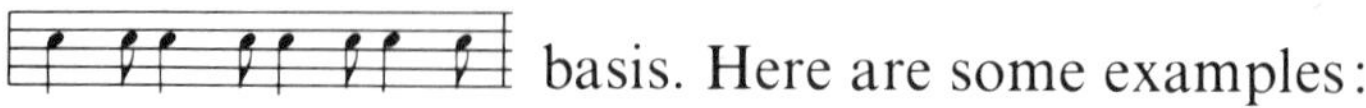 basis. Here are some examples:

By working carefully through the procedure I've outlined, you should be able to work out accurately the rhythmic pattern of the notes of your melody. It does take a lot of practice to be able to deduce phrases like

though, and because of the nature of this book I cannot coach you through the more difficult examples, only give you the facts and procedural hints and hope you can work it out thereafter! But bear this in mind—firstly, rock music is often extremely sophisticated in its use of rhythm, comparing in complexity to 'difficult' classical pieces . . .blah blah yawn . . . Mixolydian mode . . . Mike Oldfield—The New Stravinsky . . . etc, etc (snore) . . . so if you *can* notate it, you're in business. Secondly, there is *no* melody which cannot be accurately written down; it is simply a question of eliminating possibilities, my dear Whatsit. (One notable exception currently causing eminent musicologists to tear at their beards with frustration is my new composition *God's Breakfast*. This employs a time signature of 42 over infinity in a universe where time is perceived as elastic, and suitable symbols have yet to be devised to notate it.)

Let us now turn our communal mind to the *rest* signs which denote pause, cease, a welcome respite from din. May I remind you of their appearance:

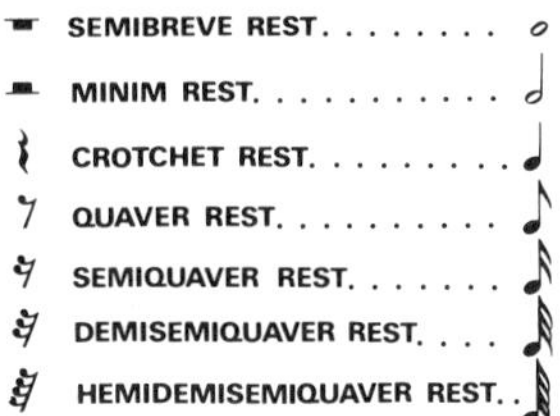

The first one ▬ doubles as an all-purpose whole bar's

rest sign: 5/4 ▬ | 4/4 ▬ | 6/8 ▬ | ETC.

Most melodies will use rests at some point and it is as well to be familiar with how to draw them. One of the commonest, the crotchet rest, is quite

difficult to draw. Here's how *I* do it: 1 2 3 4

The Americans (in typical bland fashion) have begged the question by substituting the symbol 𝄿 but I much prefer 𝄽 . (There again, I also preferred farthings, halfpennies, pence and shillings, but would they listen to me?)

It is worth noting that rests are always written in the middle of the stave even though the melody might tend to occupy a high or low register, eg

You will find that there are often alternative ways of depicting the same rhythm. We've seen one example of this already in the figures on page 70, the following example shows three different ways of writing a fairly simple phrase.

I suppose the 'correct' way would have to be no. 2, as it shows where the beat falls in relation to the played notes.

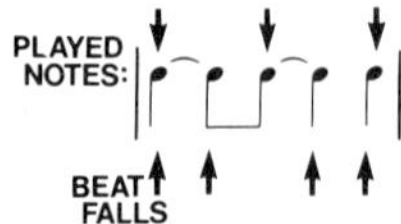

To do this, however, it has to employ more symbols than no. 1, which might to some minds seem the simplest way of writing the pattern. No. 3 is a sort of compromise between 1 and 2. To some extent, you have to follow your nose to know which alternative might render your melody clearest, but eventually I'm sure you will develop an instinct for the right combination of symbols. Everyone's brain works slightly differently and what appears clear and obvious to one person might utterly confuse another, which is why I am not prepared to say there's a 'right' or 'wrong' system.

A variation of examples 1, 2 and 3 would be as follows:

Though the three notes fall in the same places, their length has been changed; before, they ran smoothly together, but now the introduction of rests has made each one shorter and the overall effect is therefore more jerky. This type of phrasing would undoubtedly please a drummer, to whom ties are anathema . . . the reason for this is quite hard to explain, but has to do with the fact that drummers do not regard the sounds they make as having any controllable sustain. Once a drum is struck the drummer no longer wants to think about the 'note' he has created, which will swiftly die away of its own accord. His sole concern is, 'When do I hit the *next* drum?' or, more commonly, 'Where's the bar?'

When you are checking a melody for its rhythmic accuracy, keep an eye on the total amount of beats indicated in a bar. In any bar of $\frac{4}{4}$, you're allowed a maximum of four crotchets (= eight quavers = 16 semiquavers) so if you found a bar that looked like this:  within a tune

that you'd previously decided was in $\frac{4}{4}$, something would be amiss. This particular example (work it out) adds up to nine quavers, so therefore cannot be a $\frac{4}{4}$ bar. It could be a $\frac{9}{8}$ bar, but within the context of a tune in $\frac{4}{4}$ I think it more likely to be a mistake.

 would be acceptable.

When rests are involved it can be a bit difficult working out how many beats are in fact indicated within a bar. The total has to tally with the time signature of the bar, though! I'd like to set you the teeniest of exam-ettes as a reward for being such patient readers. Scrutinise the bars below and mark those which don't add up correctly. I am going out of the room for 20 minutes and when I come back I want those answers on my desk. Anyone who can't work it out will be promptly frogmarched to the gym, flicked with wet towels and shoved head first down the toilet.

ANSWERS

1. WRONG
2. WRONG
3. RIGHT
4. RIGHT
5. RIGHT
6. RIGHT
7. RIGHT
8. WRONG
9. WRONG
10. WRONG
11. RIGHT
12. WRONG
13. WRONG
14. WRONG
15. RIGHT
16. RIGHT
17. RIGHT
18. RIGHT
19. RIGHT
20. RIGHT
21. WRONG
22. RIGHT

13 Writing it Down III

Dismiss it if you will as the desperate ravings of a drunken hack, but there are certain *commercial* advantages inherent in the ability to write down music . . . like me, you could earn money in those lean periods between hit singles by writing what are known as 'lead sheets'—this is simply the top line of a song plus lyrics and chords written out in manuscript form. Music publishers need a lead sheet to protect their copyright when dealing with untrustworthy foreign agents, and *you* could be the one to provide it. Rates are negotiable (I can't tell you what I charge or else I'll be hounded by our Dept of Health and Social Security) and as long as you have broad musical taste, that is to say, can cope with playing two bars of a Johnny Moped song over and over again to determine a particularly eccentric note, this could bring you in a hitherto undreamt of amount to spend.

You may prefer to stick to writing out your own songs, however. This is arguably a good deal more satisfying than pondering for hours over LPs by the McBalls Brothers trying to decipher the Gaelic lyrics, and of course it protects your copyright and ownership of the song as efficiently as a tape. Sold? Hooked? Now read on . . .

Some final points about writing music down: you may have been wondering why sometimes a note is written  and at other times

The general rule is to put the note stems up for the lower half of the stave () and down for the upper half of the stave () so that the notes are visually pulled towards the centre of the stave.

Exceptions occur when note tails are joined:  not 

and when two lines of music are written on the same stave;

but the main thing to remember is never to write  or 

otherwise the ghosts of Stravinsky and Glenn Miller will suddenly materialise over your manuscript paper, leering and blowing raspberries in close harmony.

A last word on key signatures—if your melody employs a number of *accidentals* (sharps and flats) and these recur throughout, you can save yourself the trouble of writing them in each time they occur by employing

a key signature at the start of the tune: 

Music in a minor key can be written using the key signature of the *relative major*—for example, C major is the 'relative major' key of A minor,

and the two share the same scale 

(no accidentals). If you prefer, A minor is the relative minor of C major. The relative minor of G major is E minor, and the two share the same key

signature: 

Similarly, D minor is the relative minor of F major, and this key

signature  serves for both: 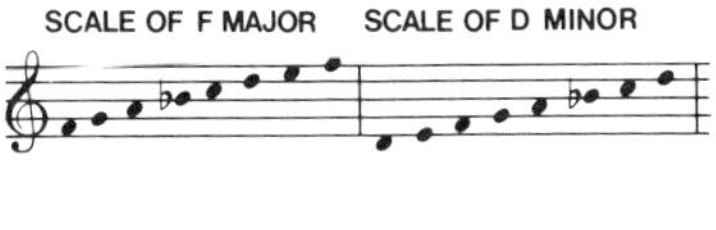

Here is a repeat of the earlier table of (major) key signatures, this time with the relative minors appended:

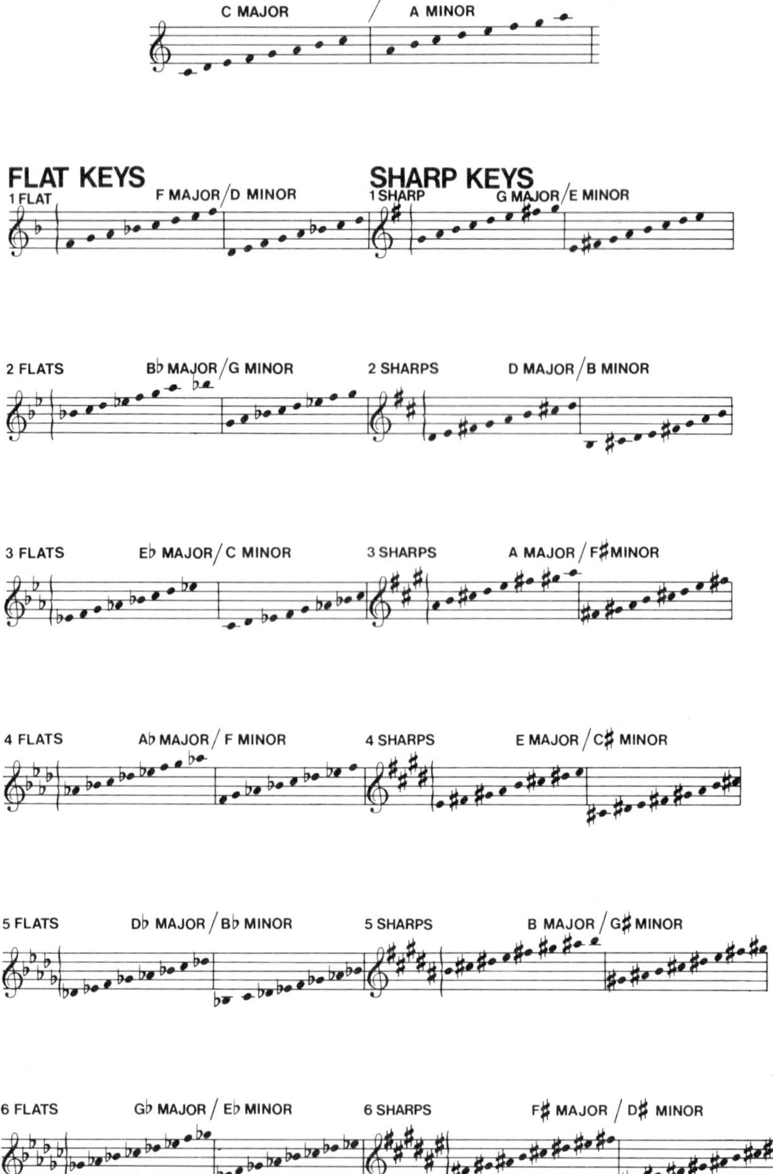

As you can see, the relative minor key is always a minor 3rd down from the major key.

After a while, the recognition of, say, four flats being A♭ major, or three sharps A major, becomes automatic. But until that point is reached you might like to consider the following formula for working out key signatures:

In sharp keys, the last sharp given is always one semitone below the key note.

In flat keys, the last flat is always a perfect fourth above the key note.

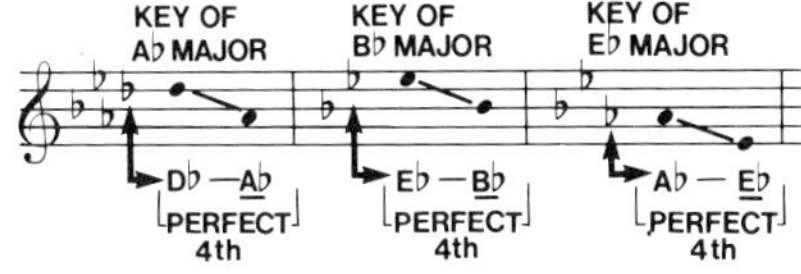

You will have noticed that the key signatures 'build up' through a cycle of fifths; flat or sharp signs are added at each step to build up a logical visual representation of the accidentals.

Having said all this, if you find it easier initially to *omit* the key signature and add sharps or flats as and when they occur, by all means do so. This is not 'correct' procedure, but when you are still struggling to tell an F from a G it can often be confusing to have to remember previous instructions concerning sharps and flats as well. On a more advanced level, you may write music which tends not to stay in any one key, and rather than be continually changing key signature you may prefer to mark individual accidentals.

Try not to chop and change between sharps and flats like this:

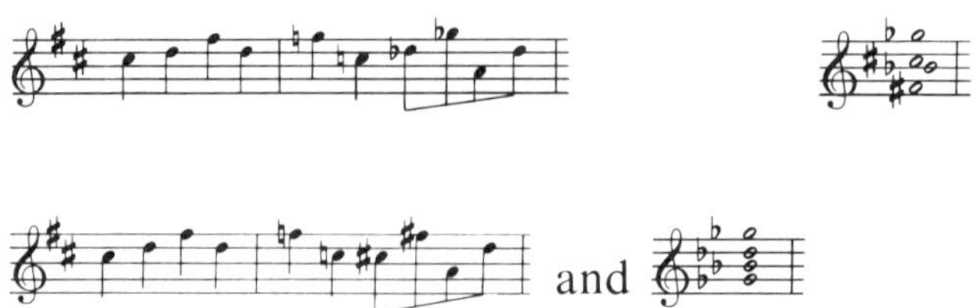

are much easier to read. Also, always leave room for the accidental in front

of the note: 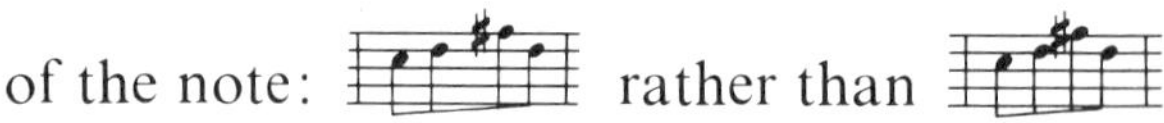

By now you should have acquired enough information to write down a melody of your own. If the 'chordal accompaniment' (assuming there is one) is simple enough to be reduced to symbols, it can be written in *above* the

melody: 

This is the sort of thing you may have seen on *sheet music* (a term given by the French to music they dislike). A change of chord within the bar can be indicated clearly by aligning each chord with its corresponding melody

note, 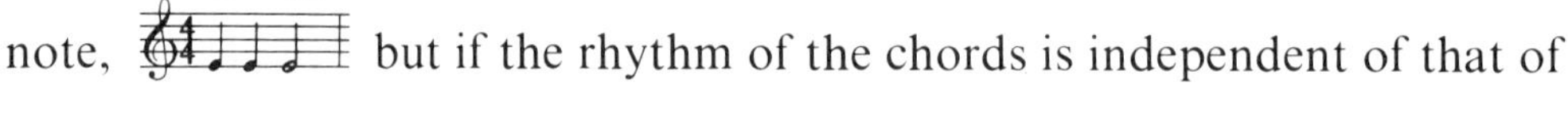

the melody, it may be necessary to separately indicate the chords' rhythm.

When you get to this level of vertical density of information, perhaps with lyrics written in underneath too, it becomes necessary to use 10 stave (or less) manuscript paper, as with 12 or more staves per page there is not quite enough room to get everything in without colliding with other staves!

14 Writing for Non-Rock Instruments

To conclude this masterpiece I must add some unpalatable facts concerning clefs and transposition.

So far, we've used two sorts of clefs, the treble 𝄞 and the bass 𝄢.

Knowing that most of you only bought this book to look at the pictures, I've included this beautiful diagram to remind you of the function of these clefs:

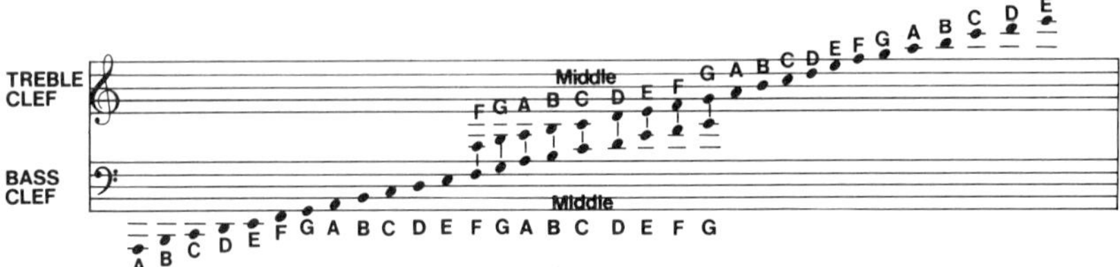

There is one further type of clef. It looks like this 𝄡 and has two positions on the stave. In the first 𝄡 it is called the *alto* clef, and in the second 𝄡 it becomes the *tenor* clef. As you can see, the centre of the clef brackets a line 𝄡 ← and in doing so, designates this line to the middle C. So, with the alto clef, middle C is here 𝄡 and with the tenor, here: 𝄡

This gives us the following series of notes:

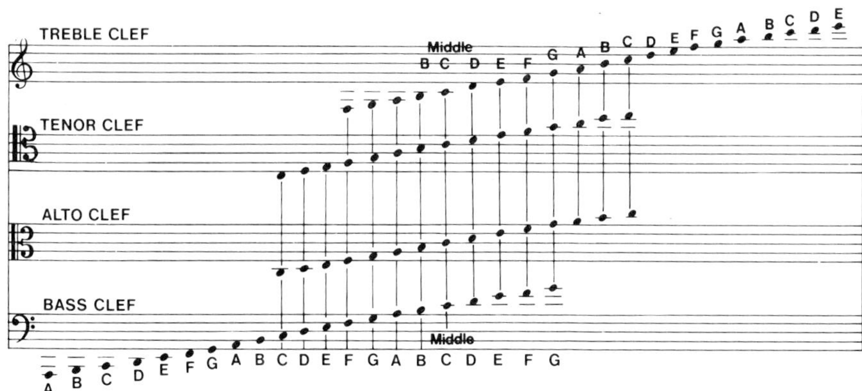

This may strike some of you as particularly zany, especially if you are still struggling with the treble and bass clefs. Why bring in a third clef when you can write any note you need on the treble or bass clef? Well, there are instruments whose range is such that parts written for them tend to lurk in the area around middle C. A good example is the viola—its range is from

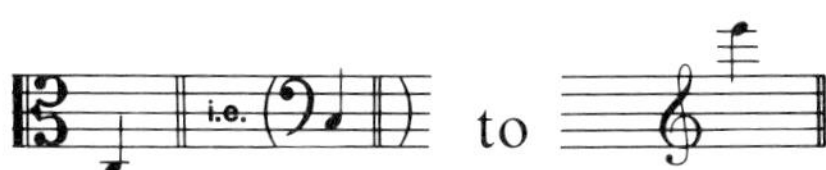

and a typical part might look something like this:

This, once the alto clef has been mastered, is a lot easier to read (and write) than

The idea when writing for any instrument is to keep all the notes (as far as possible) within the span of one clef, so as to avoid confusing the reader with continually swapping clefs or an excessive use of leger lines. I'm sure you'll agree that looks a lot more natural

and flowing than 

The alto and tenor clefs therefore offer us a bit more flexibility in our visual positioning of notes, and are essentially no more 'difficult' than the treble and bass clefs once you have grasped their basic principle.

Instruments which use the alto and tenor clefs include viola (alto clef), cello (tenor clef for high notes) and bassoon (tenor clef for highest notes), but, playing guitar, keyboards, bass or drums, you will not be affected by them. However, I mention them because I want to get on to the 'non-rock' instruments and the business of *transposing*.

If you write songs I daresay you have at moments fantasised over the possibility of hearing them performed with lush orchestral accompaniment, or at least some type of instrumental augmentation beyond the facilities of a normal four- or five-piece rock group. What you need, of course, is 'session men'—in Britain this particular class of sound-production anthropoid will stagger, in exchange for pocket-sized colour portraits of Her Majesty, on to the train at New Malden, arrive at your studio, rehearsal room or home, and there make noise under your direction. (For other countries, substitute your own currency and favourite disgusting suburb.)

In order to successfully engage the services of these individuals in dark overcoats you need lots of CASH, but also an understanding of how to write parts for them. If you prefer, a professional arranger can take care of this sort of thing for you, but I think it is much more fun and cheaper to learn to do it yourself. That way, you learn something about instruments and their sound, and how they can fit with your music. Besides, arrangers may be extremely good at their craft, but the chances are they will not have the same special insight as yourself when it comes to actually realising the sound you have in mind. As I've said several times before, *you* are the expert on your own music. Your ideas on arrangement may be naïve or embryonic, but all the same they are *your* ideas, and different from other people's notions in small but important ways. Every aspect of the sound should be under your control, so be prepared to at least have a stab at arranging for yourself—decide what instruments you want to use, work out what notes you want them to play, then write a part for each individual instrument. To begin to be able to do this there are two main things you need to know: **1** the range of the instrument, **2** whether or not it is a *transposing* instrument.

A transposing instrument is one which produces notes at a different pitch from those indicated on paper. A simple example (and one which we have already dealt with fairly painlessly) is the guitar; as you know, the bottom

E string of that instrument is written 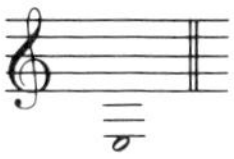 but the actual pitch it

produces is

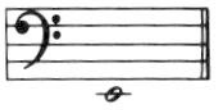

We transpose the note up an octave to keep guitar parts on the treble clef.

Bass guitar is the same; we write 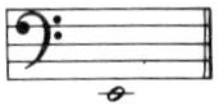 for the bottom E string, but

the pitch it produces is

This transposition avoids the use of lots of leger lines below the stave.

Now there are certain other instruments which transpose differently. A B♭ clarinet, for example, is constructed so that the simplest scale to finger gives a B♭ major scale (hence the name 'B♭ clarinet'). This is the 'natural scale' of the instrument, equivalent to the scale of C major on piano. To make life easier for clarinettists, their parts are transposed *up a tone*. This

means that a written note of 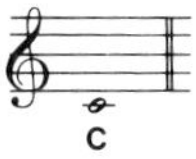 C will sound as (B♭)

Players still think of the note as a C, so when they see a C on paper they'll play on their instruments the note that they call C; but they know (unless they are complete buffoons) that the *actual pitch* produced is B♭, a tone lower than their written notes. (The actual pitch produced is referred to as *concert pitch.*)

Confusing, eh? Another example which I could and will mention is the French Horn. (Not to be confused with the Swiss Roll.) This instrument is in F, in other words, it produces pitches a perfect fifth lower than those written. A written note of 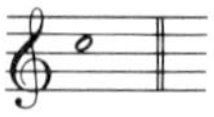 (C) will produce a pitch of  (F) therefore all French Horn parts have to be written a perfect fifth higher than the desired pitch.

I feel an irrational desire to apologise to you for this alarming phenomenon—I realise it is difficult to grasp at first, but you appreciate that it is not my fault. It *can* be very confusing, though . . . having done a few gigs with woodwind and brass players (see autobiography *My Vast Contribution To World Culture* Vols I-XIII, reasonably priced at only 85 guineas, for further details) I can remember all too painfully that when someone was playing a wrong note at a rehearsal, the transpositional factors made tracing it a hysterically complex task. There again, for a more experienced arranger or composer this sort of thing comes as second nature. However, a set of shambling, autistic novices like yourselves stand no chance. To end this book and to compound your dismay and misery I have compiled the following highly informative diagram which I hope might be useful . . .

TRANSPOSING INSTRUMENTS are marked ✱

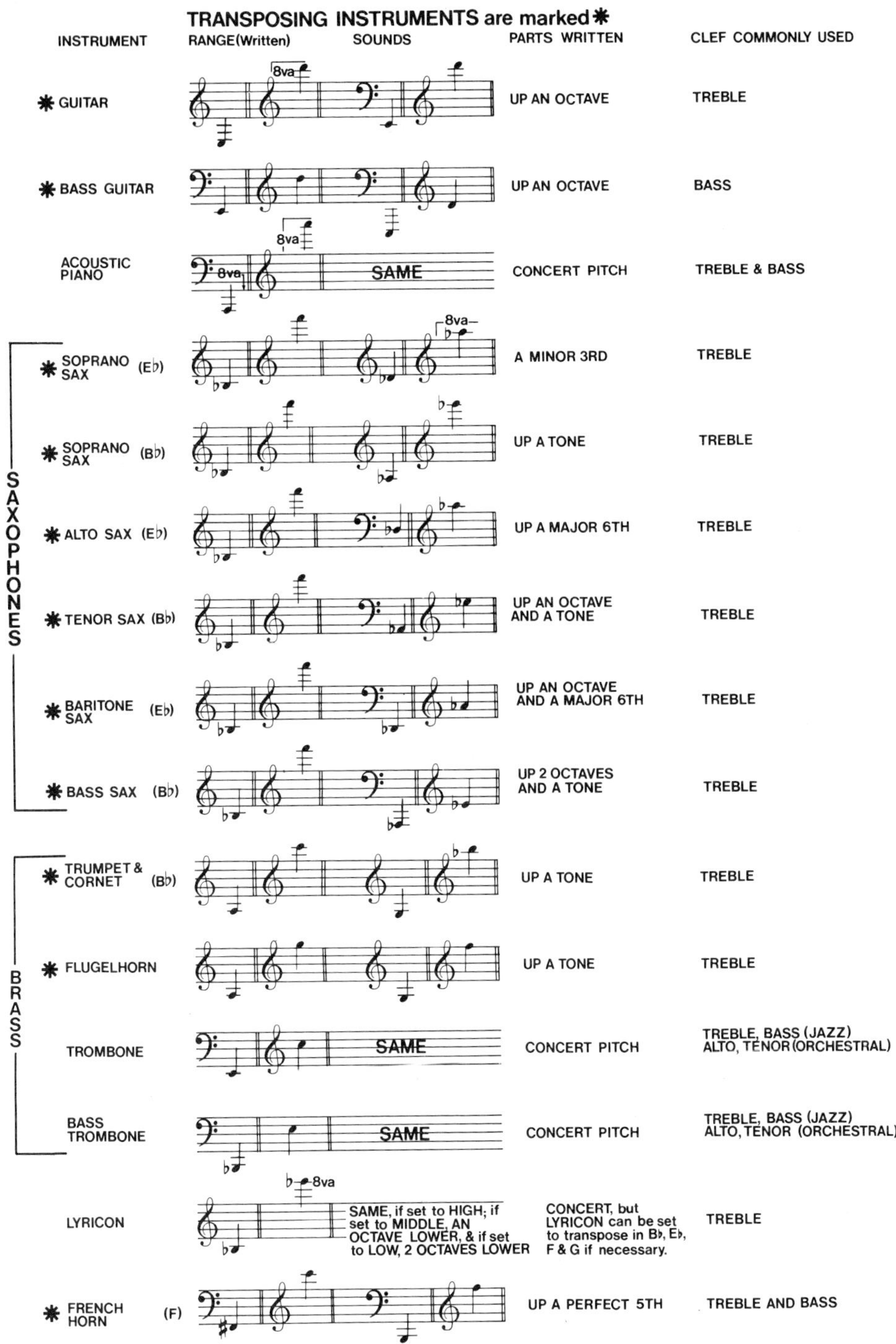

INSTRUMENT	RANGE (Written)	SOUNDS	PARTS WRITTEN	CLEF COMMONLY USED
✱ GUITAR	8va		UP AN OCTAVE	TREBLE
✱ BASS GUITAR			UP AN OCTAVE	BASS
ACOUSTIC PIANO	8va, 8va	SAME	CONCERT PITCH	TREBLE & BASS
SAXOPHONES				
✱ SOPRANO SAX (E♭)		8va	A MINOR 3RD	TREBLE
✱ SOPRANO SAX (B♭)			UP A TONE	TREBLE
✱ ALTO SAX (E♭)			UP A MAJOR 6TH	TREBLE
✱ TENOR SAX (B♭)			UP AN OCTAVE AND A TONE	TREBLE
✱ BARITONE SAX (E♭)			UP AN OCTAVE AND A MAJOR 6TH	TREBLE
✱ BASS SAX (B♭)			UP 2 OCTAVES AND A TONE	TREBLE
BRASS				
✱ TRUMPET & CORNET (B♭)			UP A TONE	TREBLE
✱ FLUGELHORN			UP A TONE	TREBLE
TROMBONE		SAME	CONCERT PITCH	TREBLE, BASS (JAZZ) ALTO, TENOR (ORCHESTRAL)
BASS TROMBONE		SAME	CONCERT PITCH	TREBLE, BASS (JAZZ) ALTO, TENOR (ORCHESTRAL)
LYRICON	8va	SAME, if set to HIGH; if set to MIDDLE, AN OCTAVE LOWER, & if set to LOW, 2 OCTAVES LOWER	CONCERT, but LYRICON can be set to transpose in B♭, E♭, F & G if necessary.	TREBLE
✱ FRENCH HORN (F)			UP A PERFECT 5TH	TREBLE AND BASS

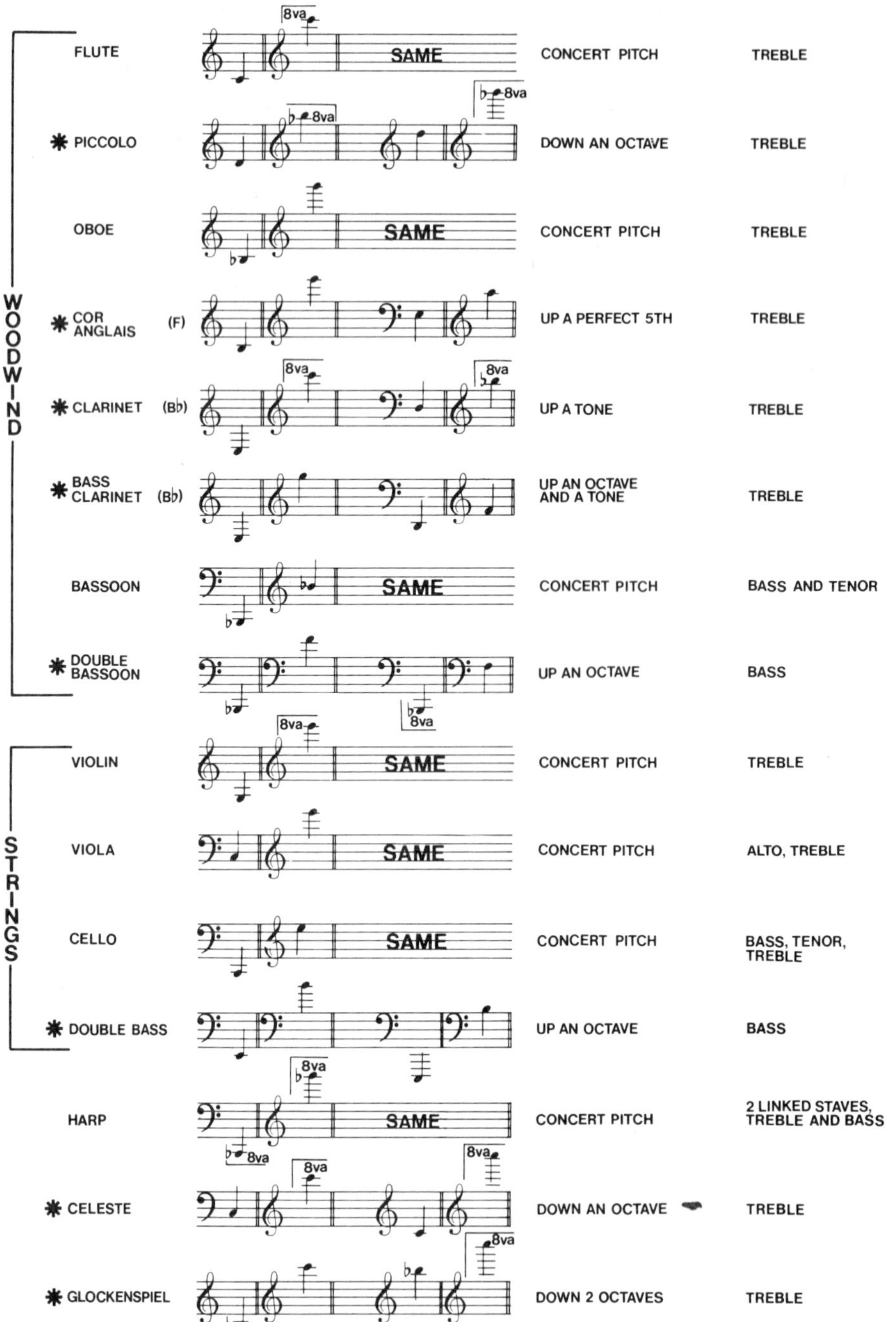

NB The ranges given are for general purposes; the upper extremities can vary a lot from player to player, especially with the sax family! If in doubt check top notes with the player you have in mind.

Dave Stewart's Scores

Hell's Bells
The Collapso
Waiting in The Wings
Borogoves
Tenemos Roads
Sample and Hold
There is No Reward

HELL'S BELLS
(Dave Stewart)
DEC '78
(N.B. 7/4 riff behind gtr. solo is based on a riff by Alan Gowen!)
(×4)
2 Minimoogs
Piano
Bass Minimoog
Minimoog Drum sound
(PINK NOISE + REPEAT)
(OSCILLATORS tuned in 4ths.)
2 M.
(OSC 2 OFF)
P.
B.M.
M.D.S.
2. M.
(OSC 2 ON)
(Ad lib)
Verses 1, 2 & 3
(×4)
(OSC 2 OFF)
Bass
Drums
H/H
SN.
B/D
OSC 2 ON
2M.
B.
D.

Minimoogs
Piano
Bass Minimoog
Bass
Drums
H/H :
SN :
B/D :
Ad lib
Repeat Verse twice.
Last time cut from *
to next section:
(OSC 2 ON)
(×3)
Play Solo
GUITAR
Ab Gb Ab Gb Bb B
SN:
Guitar
1+2
3
(×2)
Break
E D E
G.
P.
B.
D.
D F# G
E D E
D F# G
(×3)
(Rhythm)
C#maj
(+Ad lib a bit)
F (staccato)
½ TIME ROCK

Guitar
(RHYTHM)
F#m
Dmaj
Emaj
C#maj
Piano
Bass
F#m
(STACCATO)
D
(%)
E
(%)
F
(%)
Drums
G.
F#m
D
A
P.
B.
D.
Guitar
(×3)
(Note is struck once then dies away)
2 Minimoogs
(OSC 2 ON)
Piano
Minimoog Bass
(Ad lib)
Bass
(Note is struck once then dies away)
2 Minimoogs
Piano
Minimoog Bass
(Ad lib)
Repeat Verse 1, Then repeat 1st. 4 bars of Verse 1 round & fade....

THE COLLAPSO
(Dave Stewart 1977)
1
GTR.
ORGAN
PIANET
BASS
(×2)
(GUITAR)
(STEEL DRUM)
(×3)
GLISS
S.D.
GTR:
(fuzz)
A
ORG.
GTR.
PIANET
BASS
Bb
Ab6
(etc. . . .)
F
Eb6
G
F6
D
C6
Esus4
B
A6
F#
E6
G#sus4
G#
D#
Gsus4
Gm
P.
B.
O.
E
D6
F#sus4
C#
(Gb)
(×4)
(fuzz off)

GTR.
ORG.
P.
G.
(NOISE)
O.
B.
(+organ pedal)
(fuzz)

GTR.
ORG.
PIANET
BASS
G.
O.
P.
B.
(x3)
PIANET
(fuzz off)
(b)
GLISS

'THE COLLAPSO' Contd.
4
GTR.
PIANET
BASS
G.
GLISS.
P.
B.
(1st.)
(2nd.)
(ORGAN)
O.
E. PIANO
(legato)
E. PNO.
C (ad lib.)
E.P.

GTR.
ORG.
BASS
G.
ORG.
B.
G.
O.
PIANET
(fuzz)
B.
G.
O.
P.
(fuzz ff)
B.
G.
O.
P.
B.
G.
E.P.
(8va)
B.

ORG.
PIANET
GTR.
BASS
THIS PATTERN REPEATS 3 TIMES UNDER KEYBD. TUNE
O.
P.
O.
P.
E.PNO
G.
B.
8va
E.P.
G.
B.
THIS PATTERN PLAYED TWICE MORE UNDER KEYBD. TUNE
E.P.

'THE COLLAPSO' Contd.
7
E. PNO.
GTR.
BASS
E.P.
G.
B.
8va
ORG
PLANET
THIS PATTERN
PLAYED 9 TIMES
UNDER KEYBD. TUNE
O.
P.

'THE COLLAPSO' Contd.
8
ORG.
(fuzz)
(fuzz off)
PIANET
(fuzz off)
GTR.
8va
BASS
(NOISE)
O.
P.
(C#)
(fuzz)
(A#)
G.
B.
(BASS SOLO . . . . .
(Ab)
(F)
repeat section A (with continuing bass solo for 8 bars), end on
*

WAITING IN THE WINGS
(Dave Stewart)
JUNE 1981
1
VOICE
PIANO
(Intro)
4
(Verse 1)
THERE'S A WORLD OF EX-PEC — TA — TION
THAT HOLDS US CLOSE
AF—TER ALL THE SHOU — TING'S DIED A-WAY
THERE MUST BE SOME — THING LEFT FOR US TO SAY
WAI — TING HERE I WATCH YOU FACE THE CROWD A-LONE
YOUR FI — NEST HOUR IS YET TO COME
(Middle)
PROPHET
MOOG BASS
GLISS.

'WAITING IN THE WINGS' Contd.
2
VOICE
PROPHET
PIANO
MOOG BASS
STAND BY YOU
GLISS.
(Chorus)
YOU ARE MY FRIEND
(GLISS)
WHAT
8ve
E-VER YOU SAY AND DO
WHEN
(SAME PARTS AS ABOVE)
GROUP
O-THERS ALL DROP A-WAY
I WILL
AL-WAYS STAND BY YOU
AND I

'WAITING IN THE WINGS' (Contd.)
3
VOICE
PROPHET
PIANO
MOOG BASS
8ve
(GLISS.)
CAN'T HELP WORRYING 'BOUT YOU WHAT
E-VER YOU SAY AND DO 'COS
GROUP
(SAME PARTS AS ABOVE)
YOU ARE MY FRIEND AND I'LL
AL-WAYS STAND BY YOU
(Verse 2)
THE BOOK YOU LENT ME TOLD ME LOTS FOR SURE
THE LOOK YOU GAVE ME TELLS ME SO MUCH MORE
YOUR DAR-KEST HOUR IS YET TO COME
(ETC.)
Repeat MIDDLE
Repeat 1st. ½ of CHORUS

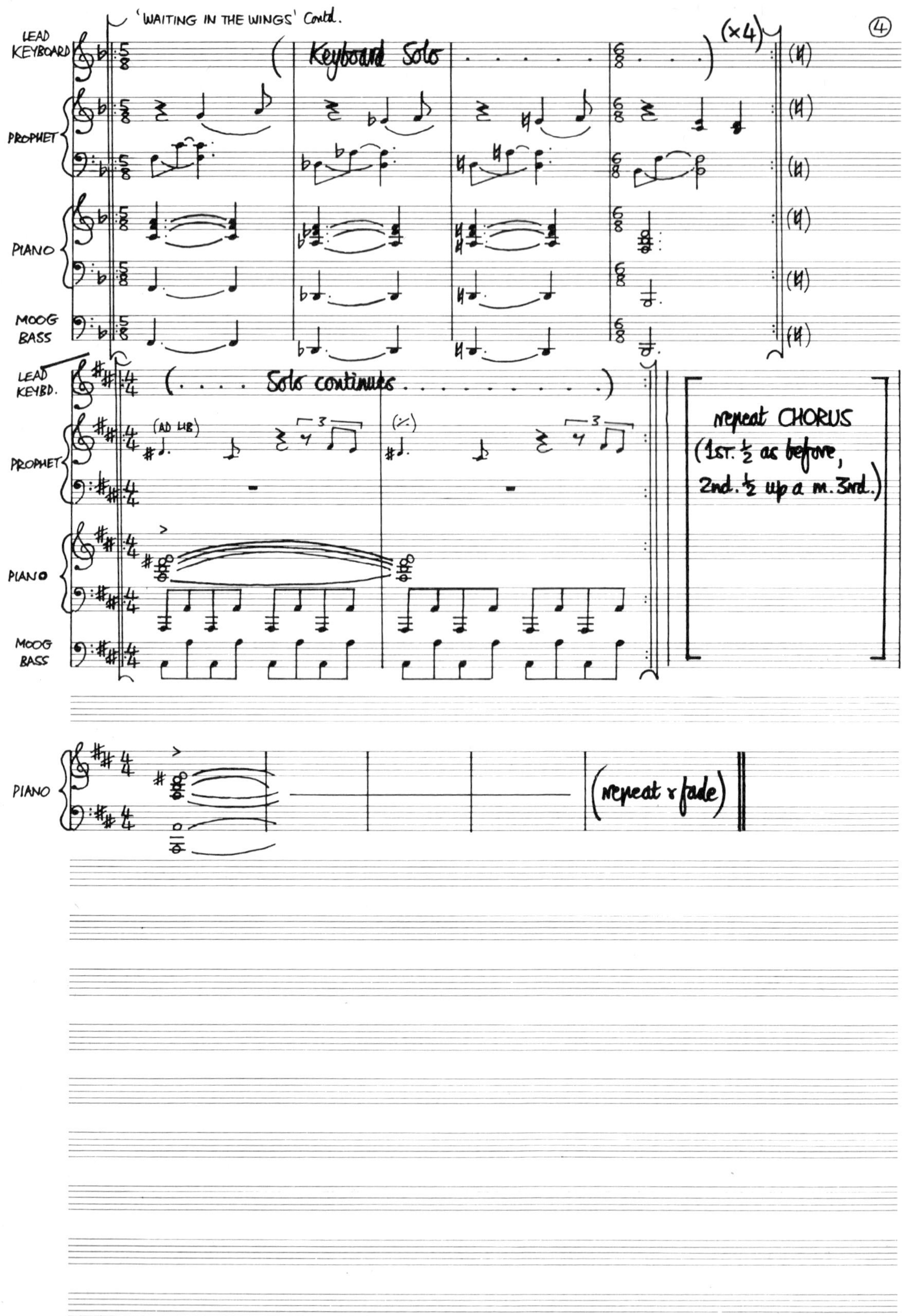
'WAITING IN THE WINGS' Contd.
LEAD KEYBOARD
PROPHET
PIANO
MOOG BASS
Keyboard Solo
(×4)
LEAD KEYBD.
Solo continues
(AD LIB)
repeat CHORUS
(1st. ½ as before,
2nd. ½ up a m. 3rd.)
PIANO
(repeat & fade)

Part One.

ORG.
SYNTH.
PNO.
BASS

GTR.
(ORG)
(SYNTH.)
(PNO.)
(BASS)

VOICE
(GTR)
crescendo.
dim.
(ORG)
[Eb M7]
[Cm11]
(SYNTH)
simile (8va's)
PNO.
(PNO)
(BASS)

B L.H.
Ab L.H.
F L.H.
SYNTH.

VOICE
GTR
PNO.
BASS
8va

8va

'BOROGOVES' Contd.

6
ad lib.
(8va)
(b)
(♮)

(ad. lib. fill)
8va
TR
(TRILLS CONTINUE A SEMITONE BELOW WRITTEN NOTE)
(Ad lib)
(Ad lib.........)
F (ad lib)
E (ad lib)
→ (over)

(Ad lib. to fit with B♮7 chord)
8va
8va
Gm9♮7
arpeggios...
(Gm9♮7)
arpeggios...
(Gm9♮7)

TENEMOS ROADS
(Dave Stewart 1976)
1
Moogs (or Woodwind)
dim.
Organ
Pianet
(fuzz)
(continue semiquavers)
Bass
Drums
Moog / Fuzz guitar
Organ
Pianet
Bass
Drums
DIM.
ORGAN OVERDUB 2nd. TIME ONLY
M./F.G.
O.
P.
B.
D.

Moog/Fuzz guitar
Organ
Pianet
Bass
Drums
2nd.
1st.
M./F.G.
O.
P.
B.
D.
(⁒ SEMIQUAVERS CONTINUE ⁒)
1
FUZZ ORGAN OVERDUB
2
(⁒ SEMIQUAVERS CONTINUE . . .
Guitar
Moog
(fuzz)
El. piano 2
(⁒ SEMIQUAVERS CONTINUE . . .)
(fuzz ff)
8va
(Round till signal from organ)
(×16)
(×4)
Abm
G
Ab♮7
El. piano 2
SOLO IN Abm
SOLO (CONTD.) IN G
(⁒)
(IN Ab♮7)
Ab
SOLO
(Dm)
(⁒)
(Eb♮7)
(⁒ SEMIQUAVERS CONTINUE)
etc.

'TENEMOS ROADS' Contd.
3
(... solo continues)
Guitar
Organ
Pianet
Bass
Drums
(Eb△7)
(Bb△7)
G.
O.
P.
B.
D.
(Gm9)
(Ab△7)
(etc.)
(⁒ SEMIQUAVERS CONTINUE)
(Cm)
(N.B. Moog can double organ top line from here to end of guitar solo)
(Db△7)
(F#m)
(Amaj)
Moog
Gtr.
Organ
Pianet
M.
O.
P.

Voice
Guitar
Moog/ El. Piano 2
Organ
Pianet
Bass
Drums
FROM THE
CRADLE
TO THE
GRAVE
(fuzz)
(MOOG)
(EL. PIANO)
8va
V.
G.
(EL. Piano 2)
(Organ)
(Pianet)
B.
D.
THERE ARE ROADS FOR US
ALL
THAT WE'LL
(sus.)
FIND
AND
FO — LLOW
TO
THE
END
E.P. 2
O.
P.
LEADING
(MOOG)
EL. PIANO
(Ad lib. rhythm)
(loco)
(fuzz)

Voice
Guitar
Moog / El. Piano 2
El. Piano 1
Bass
Drums
UP-WARDS TO A PLACE IN THE STARS
TEN MILL-ION MILES A-WAY
(MOOG)
(fuzz ff)
V.
G.
E.P. 2
E.P. 1
B.
D.
(EL. PIANO)
8va
THERE'S A
(8va)
F♯/E (AD LIB. ARPEGGIOS)
(semiquavers continue)
PATH CALLED TENEMOS ROADS
EV-ERY THING HAP-PENING
THERE IS HIS-TO-RY RE-CORDS OF A-GES BE-FORE WE WERE BORN BUT THE
Moog
(MOOG)

Voice
Guitar
Moog/ El. Piano 2
El. Piano 1
Bass
Drums
SOUND OF MEN IN BAT—TLE MAKES ME CRY OUT IN MY DREAM
(EL. PIANO)
(+ AD LIB. ARPEGGIOS (G/F))
(8va)
V.
G.
E.P. 2
E.P. 1
B.
D.
(% SEMIQUAVERS CONTINUE)
(L.H.)
8va
HEARING THE SOUNDS OF BAT—TLE FAR A— WAY
AND THE TRUM—
(MOOG (16'))

Voice
Guitar
El. piano 2
Moog
El. piano 1
Bass
Drums
PETS CALL—ING MARKS THE END OF THEIR TIME OF PEACE IN TENE—MOS
ROADS
THINGS ARE CHANG-ING DI
(Organ:)
(Pianet:)
REC TED BY THE MEN WHO TIRED OF MA—KING LOVE, MAKE
8va
WAR
(ad lib.)

SAMPLE AND HOLD (Dave Stewart / Bill Bruford)
1
(!)

8va

SAMPLE AND HOLD BASS LINE

LEAD SHEET
THERE IS NO REWARD
(Dave Stewart)
1
KEYBOARD:
(×4)
(. . . . KEYBOARD ARPEGGIO continues)
(Verse 1) RIGHT FROM THE START BE-FORE YOU'VE
E—VEN LEARNED THE AL-PHA-BET OFF BY HEART
D9 Bm9 G9 Em (D9 no 3rd.)
THEY'VE MA—NAGED TO CLAIM YOUR DAY
(ARPEGGIO resumes. . . .)
YOU CAN GO TO SCHOOL YOU CAN
GO TO WORK AND DO THINGS YOU DON'T WANT TO THERE'LL BE
D9 Bm9 G9 Em D9(no 3rd.)
TALK OF ACHIEVEMENT AND HA—PPI—NESS A—LONG THE WAY
(ARPEGGIO resumes. . . .)
Bbmaj7/D
(Middle) BUT FOR ALL THE TIME YOU'RE BORED
Am7/E F9 Bbmaj7/D
AND SIT-TING ROUND FEELING IGNORED
Bbmaj7 Abmaj7 Cmaj7/9 Dmaj7/9
BASS: C E F F#
A Bb B D E D
(Chorus) THERE IS NO RE—WARD THEY'RE NOT GI—VING

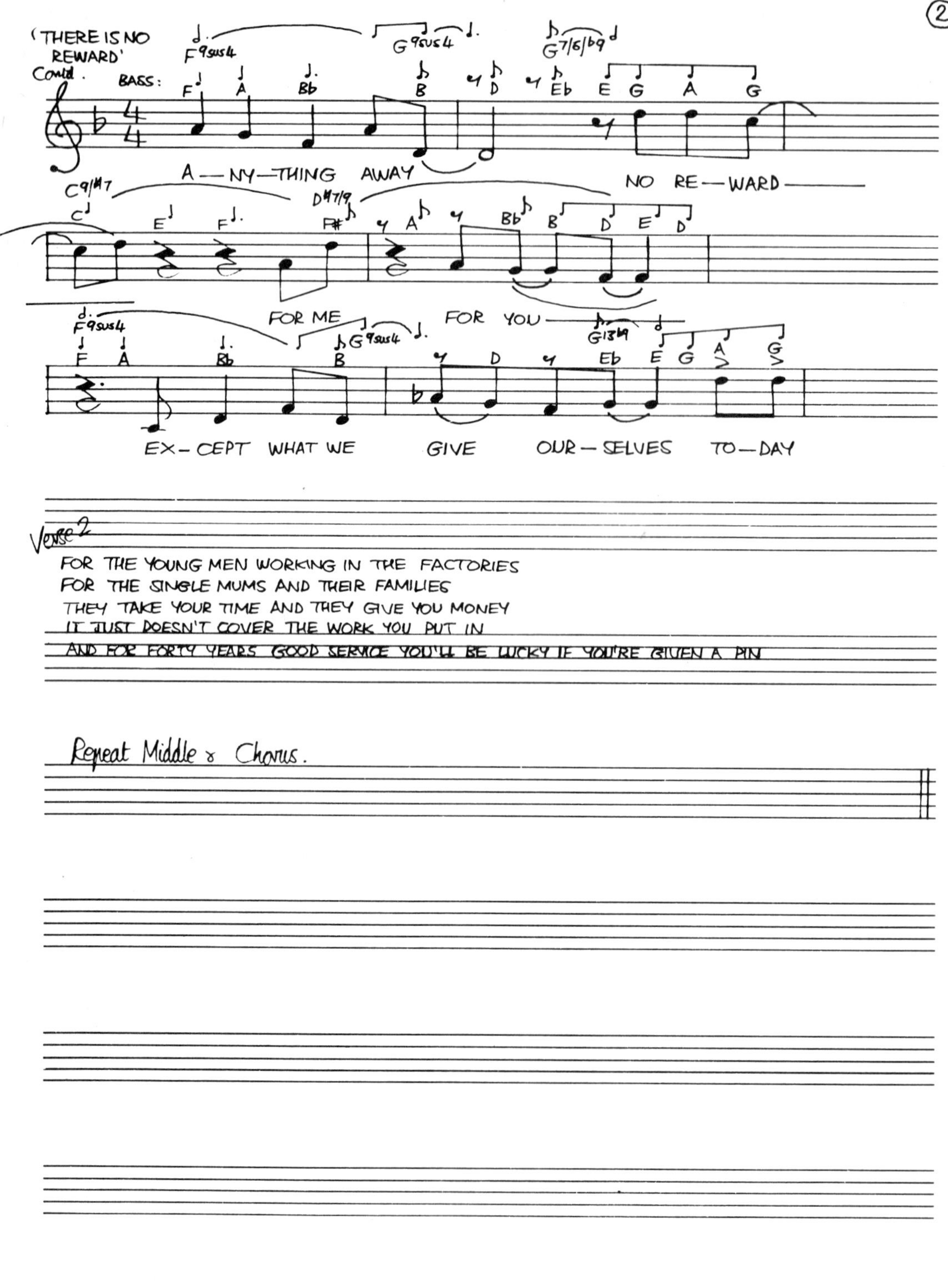

2
('THERE IS NO REWARD' Contd.
BASS:
F9sus4
G9sus4
G7/6/b9
F A Bb B D Eb E G A G
A — NY — THING AWAY
NO RE — WARD
C9/#7
D#7/9
C E F F# A Bb B D E D
FOR ME
FOR YOU
F9sus4
G9sus4
G13b9
F A Bb B D Eb E G A G
EX — CEPT WHAT WE GIVE OUR — SELVES TO — DAY
Verse 2
FOR THE YOUNG MEN WORKING IN THE FACTORIES
FOR THE SINGLE MUMS AND THEIR FAMILIES
THEY TAKE YOUR TIME AND THEY GIVE YOU MONEY
IT JUST DOESN'T COVER THE WORK YOU PUT IN
AND FOR FORTY YEARS GOOD SERVICE YOU'LL BE LUCKY IF YOU'RE GIVEN A PIN
Repeat Middle & Chorus.

Thanks Department

Bob Emmines	drum notation
Phil Miller	guitar notes
Allan Holdsworth	guitar chord voicings
John Walters	sax info
Paul Nieman	remarks about trombones
Autographics	artwork

Thanks to Shafmere Music Ltd for permission to reprint *Hell's Bells*, *Waiting in The Wings* and *There is No Reward*; to E. G. Music for *Sample and Hold* and to Virgin Music (Publishers) Ltd for *The Collapso*, *Borogoves* and *Tenemos Roads*.